W9-BHB-320

The
Expectant
Father

—

Facts, Tips,
and Advice
for Dads-to-Be

"Just as your wife suspected, Mr. Sanders. You have a very little boy growing inside you."

The
Expectant
Father

—

Facts, Tips,
and Advice
for Dads-to-Be

Armin A. Brott and Jennifer Ash

Abbeville Press ♦ Publishers
New York ♦ Paris ♦ London

To Tirzah and Talya,
who make the world a better place.—A.A.B.

For Joe, Clarke, and my parents, Clarke and Agnes Ash,
with love and affection.—J.A.

EDITOR: Jacqueline Decter
DESIGNER: Celia Fuller
PRODUCTION EDITOR: Abigail Asher
PRODUCTION MANAGER: Lou Bilka

First hardcover edition
10 9 8 7 6 5 4 3 2

Cover photograph by Milton Heiberg. For cartoon credits, see page 215.

Library of Congress Cataloging-in-Publication Data
Brott, Armin A.
    The expectant father : facts, tips, and advice for dads-to-be /
Armin A. Brott and Jennifer Ash.
        p.   cm.
    Includes bibliographical references and index.
    ISBN 1-55859-690-9 (pb).—ISBN 0-7892-0417-7 (hc)
    1. Fathers—Psychology.   2. Pregnancy—Psychological aspects.
I. Ash, Jennifer.   II. Title.
HQ756.B76   1995
649'.1'0242—dc20   94-41096

Contents

Acknowledgments

Many people had a hand in creating this book and all deserve much gratitude. In particular, I'd like to thank David Cohen and Jackie Needleman, and Douglas and Rachel Arava for their careful reading of the manuscript and for their thoughtful, insightful comments and suggestions; and Michael Feiner and Jenny Shy, and Matthew and Janice Tannin for sharing their anecdotes, advice, and recipes.

Thanks also to Jackie Decter for her savvy advice and editing acumen, to Jim Levine and Arielle Eckstut for thinking of me at the right time, and especially to Jennifer Ash, whose idea made this project possible.

But by far the biggest thanks goes to my wife, Andrea Adam Brott, who read every draft, helped hone my ideas (while adding some of her own), and even managed a chuckle about the irony of our having to hire a babysitter so I could have enough time to write a book about how men can get more involved with their children. Without Andrea's love, encouragement, and support, this book wouldn't exist, and I would never have been able to enjoy the kind of relationship I now have with my children.

Armin A. Brott
November 1994

While awaiting the arrival of our first baby, I vowed to read every piece of printed advice on pregnancy and motherhood. It quickly became apparent that nine months wasn't sufficient time to digest all that was available for expectant mothers. However, my husband's bedside table remained bare, not for lack of interest but for want of resources. A heartfelt thanks to Joe, who convinced me men do want to know more about pregnancy and thus encouraged me to embark on this project. I'm also grateful to my brothers, Eric and Jim, and to the many friends who candidly discussed impending fatherhood and made insightful suggestions. Virginia Webb's and Esther Williams's advice about newborns was invaluable.

Sincere thanks to everyone at Abbeville, especially Alan Mirken, who supported this project from the onset. The enthusiasm of Bob Abrams and Mark Magowan kept it on track. Jackie Decter deftly guided the book to completion and her friendship made the journey a joy. Thanks to Armin Brott for agreeing to provide the narrative, which breathed male life into the book. Laura Straus made the inclusion of cartoons possible, and Celia Fuller's inspired design brought all of this to life.

Jennifer Ash
November 1994

Introduction

When my wife and I got pregnant in July 1989, I was the happiest I'd ever been. That pregnancy, labor, and the birth of our first daughter was a time of incredible closeness, tenderness, and passion. Long before we'd married, my wife and I had made a commitment to share equally in raising our children. And it seemed only natural that the process of shared parenting should begin during pregnancy.

Since neither of us had had children before, we were both rather ill-prepared for pregnancy. Fortunately for my wife, there were literally hundreds of books designed to educate, encourage, support, and comfort women during their pregnancies. But when I began to realize that I, too, was expecting, and that the pregnancy was bringing out feelings and emotions I didn't understand, I couldn't find any books to turn to. I looked for answers in my wife's pregnancy books, but information about what expectant fathers go through (if it was dis-cussed at all) was at best superficial, consisting mostly of advice on how men could be supportive of their pregnant wives. And to make things worse, since my wife and I were the first couple in our circle of close friends to get preg-nant, there was no one else I could talk to about what I was going through, no one who could reassure me that what I was feeling was normal and all right.

Until fairly recently, there has been precious little research on the man's emotional and psychological experiences during pregnancy. The very title of one of the first articles to appear on the subject should give you some idea of the medical and psychiatric communities' attitude toward the impact of preg-nancy on men. Written by William H. Wainwright, M.D., and published in the July 1966 issue of the *American Journal of Psychiatry*, it was called "Father-hood as a Precipitant of Mental Illness."

But as you'll soon find out, an expectant father's experience during the transition to fatherhood is not confined simply to excitement—or mental illness; if it were, this book would never have been written. The reality is that men's emotional response to pregnancy is no less varied than women's; expectant fathers feel everything from relief to denial, fear to frustration, anger to joy. And for anywhere from 22 to 79 percent of men, there are physical symptoms of pregnancy as well (more on this on pages 53–55).

So why haven't men's experiences been discussed more? In my opinion it's because we, as a society, value motherhood more than fatherhood, and we automatically assume that issues of childbirth and childrearing are women's issues. But as you'll learn—both from reading this book and from your own experience—this is simply not the case.

Who, Exactly, Has Written This Book?

When Jennifer Ash approached me about collaborating with her on *The Expectant Father*, we agreed that our goal was to help you understand and make sense of what you're going through during your pregnancy. That's an important goal, but one that is clearly dependent on your partner's *being* pregnant. A good understanding of your *partner's* perspective on the pregnancy—emotional as well as physical—is essential to understanding how *you* will react. It was precisely this perspective that Jennifer, whose son was born only a few days after my second daughter, provided. Throughout our collaboration she contributed valuable information and comments not only about what pregnant women are going through but also about the ways women most want men to stay involved.

A Note on Structure

Throughout the book, Jennifer and I try to present straightforward, practical information in an easy-to-absorb format. Each of the main chapters is divided into four sections as follows:

What She's Going Through
Even though this is a book about what you as an expectant father are going through during pregnancy, we felt it was important to summarize your partner's physical and emotional pregnancy experience as well.

What's Going On with the Baby

This section lets you in on your future child's progress—from sperm and egg to living, breathing infant.

What You're Going Through

This section covers the wide range of feelings—good, bad, and indifferent— you'll probably experience at some time during the pregnancy. It also describes the *physical* changes you may go through, as well as the ways the pregnancy may affect your sex life.

Staying Involved

While the "What You're Going Through" section covers the emotional and physical side of pregnancy, this section gives you specific facts, tips, and advice on what you can *do* to make the pregnancy yours as well as your partner's. For instance, you'll find easy, nutritious recipes to prepare, information on how to start a college fund for the baby, valuable advice on getting the most out of your birth classes, and tips about how to be supportive of your partner and stay included in the pregnancy.

The book covers more than the nine months of pregnancy. Jennifer and I have included a detailed chapter on labor and delivery and another on Cesarean section, both of which prepare you to understand and help your partner through the birth itself. Perhaps even more important, these chapters prepare you for the often overwhelming emotions you may experience when your partner is in labor and your child is born.

We've also included a special chapter that addresses the major questions and concerns you may have about caring for and getting to know your child after you bring him or her home. And finally, we've included a chapter called "Fathering Today," in which you'll learn to recognize—and overcome— the many obstacles contemporary fathers are likely to encounter.

As you go through the book, remember that each of us brings different emotional baggage to our pregnancies, and that none of us will react to the same situation in the same way. You may find that some of the feelings described in the "What You're Going Through" section in the third-month chapter won't really ring true for you until the fifth month, or that you have already experienced them in the first month. You may also want to try out some of the ideas and activities suggested in the "Staying Involved" sections in a different order. Feel free.

A Note on Terminology

Wife, Girlfriend, Lover . . .

In an attempt to avoid offending anyone (an approach that usually ends up offending *everyone*), we've decided to refer to the woman who's carrying the baby as "your partner."

Hospitals, Doctors . . .

We realize that not everyone who has a baby delivers in a hospital or is under the care of a medical doctor. Still, because this is the most frequent scenario, we've chosen to refer to the place where the baby will be born as "the hospital" and to the people attending the birth (besides you, of course) as "doctors," "nurses," "medical professionals," or "practitioners."

As a rule, today's fathers (and prospective fathers) want to be much more involved with their children than their own fathers were able to be. It's our belief that the first step on the road toward full involvement is to take an active role in the pregnancy. And it's our hope that when you're through reading *The Expectant Father*—which is the book Jennifer wishes she could have bought for her husband when she was pregnant and I wish I'd had both times my wife and I were pregnant—you'll be much better prepared to participate in this important new phase of your life.

The First Decisions

The first major questions you and your partner will face after learning you are pregnant are *Where are we going to have the baby?*, *Who is going to help us deliver it?*, and *How much is it all going to cost?* To a certain extent, the answers will be dictated by the terms of your insurance policy, but there are nevertheless a range of options to consider.

Where and How

Hospital Birth

For most couples—especially first-time parents—the hospital is the most common place to give birth. It's also the safest. In the unlikely event that complications arise, most hospitals have specialists on staff twenty-four hours a day and are equipped with all the necessary machinery and medications. And in those first hectic hours or days after the birth, the on-staff nurses monitor the baby and mother and help both new parents with the dozens of questions that are likely to come up. They also help fend off unwanted intrusions.

Many hospitals now have labor and delivery rooms that are decorated to look less like a hospital and more like a bedroom at home. The cozy decor is supposed to make you and your partner feel more comfortable. But with nurses dropping by every hour or so, and with tables full of sophisticated monitoring equipment and cabinets full of sterile supplies, it's hard to forget where you are.

Home Birth

With all their high-tech efficiency and stark, impersonal, antiseptic conditions, hospitals are not for everyone. So, if you don't feel particularly comfortable in

Risks of Home Birth

Things can happen during your pregnancy that might make a home birth unnecessarily risky: if your partner develops preeclampsia (pregnancy-induced hypertension, a fairly rare condition, but one that can have serious complications if not detected and treated early) or goes into labor prematurely, or if you find out that the baby is breech (feet down instead of head down) or that you're having twins (or more), you'll probably want to reconsider the hospital.

You also might want to reconsider the hospital if your partner suffers from diabetes, has a heart or kidney condition, has had hemorrhaging in a previous labor (a quick blood transfusion can be conducted at the hospital), has had a previous Cesarean section, or smokes cigarettes regularly. While plenty of people with these and other conditions have delivered perfectly healthy babies at home, the chances that complications can develop are significant, and you and your partner should make every effort to ensure the safest possible delivery.

hospitals, and you're not anticipating any complications during pregnancy, home birth can be a more relaxed option to consider.

But be prepared. Having a baby at home is quite a bit different than it's made out to be in those old westerns—you're going to need a lot more than clean towels and boiling water. If you are considering a home birth, contact a nurse-midwife who, at the very least, will be able to provide a list of the things you'll need.

My wife and I thought about a home birth for our second baby but ultimately decided against it. While I don't consider myself particularly squeamish, I just couldn't imagine how we'd avoid making a mess all over the bedroom carpet. What really clinched it for us, though, was that our first child had been an emergency Cesarean section; fearing that we might run into problems again, we opted to be near the doctors.

Natural Birth vs. Medicated

In recent years giving birth "naturally"—without drugs, pain medication, or any medical intervention—has become the most desirable method of delivery. But just because it's popular doesn't mean it's for everybody. Labor and delivery are going to be a painful experience—for both of you—and many couples elect to take advantage of the advances medical science has made in relieving the pain and discomfort of childbirth.

Be flexible. You may be planning a natural childbirth and conditions could develop that necessitate intervention or the use of medication (see pages 151–55). On the other hand, you may be planning a medicated delivery but could find yourself snowed in someplace far from your hospital and any pain medication.

Who's Going to Help?

At first glance, it may seem that your partner should be picking a medical practitioner alone—after all, *she's* the one who's going to be poked and prodded as the pregnancy develops. But considering that more than 90 percent of today's expectant fathers are present during the delivery of their children, and that the vast majority of them have been involved in some significant way during the rest of the pregnancy, *you're* probably going to be spending a lot of time with the practitioner as well. So if at all possible, you should feel comfortable with the final choice, too.

Private Obstetrician

If your partner is over twenty, she probably has been seeing a gynecologist for a few years. And since many gynecologists also do obstetrics, it should come as no surprise that most couples elect to have the woman's regular obstetrician/gynecologist (OB/GYN) deliver the baby.

Private OB/GYNs are generally the most expensive way to go, but your insurance company will usually pick up at least part of the bill. Private OBs also give their patients the most personal attention. Make sure, though, that you arrange to meet the other doctors in your OB's practice, in case the baby is born on a day when your doctor is not on call. Labor and delivery are going to be stressful enough without having to deal with a doctor you've never met before.

Midwife

Even if your partner has a regular OB, you might want to consider having a midwife deliver your baby. Midwives are specially trained in coaching women during labor and in delivering babies. Because of this training, many midwives—a good number of whom are also registered nurses—actually have more experience delivering babies than OB/GYNs.

Although midwives are not as common in the United States as they are in Europe, they're becoming increasingly popular. Many standard OB/GYN

What to Ask Your Prospective Practitioner

Before making a final decision about who's going to deliver the baby, you should get satisfactory answers to the following questions:

ESPECIALLY FOR OB/GYNS

- Do you allow family members and/or coaches to attend delivery?
- Do you recommend any particular childbirth preparation method (Lamaze, Bradley, and so on)?
- At which hospital do you deliver your babies?
- Are you board certified?
- Do you have any specialties or special training?
- How many partners do you have and how often are they on rotation?
- How many sonograms do you routinely recommend?
- Do you perform amniocentesis yourself?
- What percentage of your deliveries are Cesarean?
- Do you permit fathers to attend Cesarean sections?
- Do you routinely order medications, IV, enemas, fetal monitoring, or do you judge each situation individually?
- What is your policy on inducing labor?
- Do you usually perform an episiotomy?
- Can the mother lift the baby out herself if she wishes?

practices, recognizing that some of their patients might want to have a midwife in attendance at the birth, now have one or more on staff. Officially, then, your partner is still under the care of an M.D.—whose services can be paid for by insurance—but she'll still get the kind of care she wants. It's important to remember, though, that midwives are generally not trained to deal with birthing complications and must refer their "patients" to an M.D. if anything unusual or dangerous arises.

Many states strictly regulate the midwife's role, and midwives are frequently not allowed to do the actual delivery of the baby. If you're considering using a midwife, the American College of Nurse Midwives (see page 18) can put you in touch with one in your area and fill you in on any applicable regulations.

♦ Can the father?

♦ Do you routinely suction the baby during delivery?

♦ Do you usually hand the naked baby straight to the mother?

♦ Do you allow the mother or father to cut the umbilical cord?

ESPECIALLY FOR MIDWIVES

♦ Are you licensed?

♦ How many babies have you delivered?

♦ What M.D.s are you associated with?

♦ What position do most of the women you work with adopt for the second stage of labor?

FOR BOTH OB/GYNS AND MIDWIVES

♦ What are your rates and payment plans?

♦ What insurance, if any, do you honor?

♦ What percentage of your patients had natural, unmedicated births in the past year?

♦ Are you willing to wait until the umbilical cord has stopped pulsating before you clamp it?

♦ Can the baby be put to the breast immediately after delivery?

♦ Are you willing to dim the lights when the baby is born?

Family Physician

Your family doctor has probably delivered a few babies in his or her time. But since obstetrics isn't the focus of a family physician's practice, he or she probably doesn't know the support staff or the hospital procedures as well as the OB/GYN whose office is across the street and who delivers three babies a week there. In addition, many hospitals won't allow anyone but "recognized" OBs or midwives to admit patients to the delivery ward.

Nevertheless, if your doctor has delivered other babies in your family and you want him or her to deliver yours, it may be possible to make special arrangements. But if you go this route, make sure an OB will be around for the actual birth—just in case.

For More Information about Prenatal and Family Medical Care

American Academy of Pediatrics
141 Northwest Point Blvd.
Elk Grove Village, IL 60009
(708) 228-5005

American College of Nurse Midwives
818 Connecticut Avenue, N.W.
Washington, DC 20006
(202) 728-9860

American College of Obstetricians
and Gynecologists
409 12th Street, S.W.
Washington, DC 20024
(202) 638-5577

American Red Cross
17th & D Streets
Washington DC, 20006
(202) 737-8300

International Childbirth Education Association
8060 26th Avenue South
Bloomington, MN 55425
(612) 854-8660

Maternity Center Association
48 East 92nd Street
New York, NY. 10128
(212) 369-7300

Bills

Having a baby isn't cheap. Even if you have good insurance, the 20 percent (plus your deductible) that most policies make you pay can still add up in a hurry. In the sections that follow, you'll get an idea of how much a typical—and a not-so-typical—pregnancy and childbirth experience might cost. It's a

"Listen, are you absolutely sure you want to have kids?"

good idea to look over your insurance policy, find out about how much it will
be picking up, and start putting together a budget now.

Pregnancy and Childbirth

Most doctors will charge one flat fee for your partner's care during the entire
pregnancy. This should cover monthly visits during the first two trimesters,
biweekly visits for the next month or so, and then weekly visits until
delivery. But don't make the mistake of thinking that that's all you'll pay.
Bills for blood and urine tests, ultrasounds, hospital fees, and other procedures will work their way into your mailbox at least once a month. Here's
what you can expect to pay (before your insurance pays its part) for having
your baby:

OB/GYN

$2,500 to $6,500 for general prenatal care and a problem-free vaginal delivery. Most doctors will meet with you to discuss their rates and the services
they provide. For a list of important questions to ask, see pages 16–17. In
addition, be sure to discuss which insurance plans, if any, they participate in;

whether they'll bill your insurance company directly or will want you to make a deposit (usually about 25 percent of the anticipated bill) up front; whether you can make your payments in installments; and whether they expect their fee to be paid in full *before* the delivery.

MIDWIFE
The average cost of a delivery by a midwife is $1,200.

Lab and Other Expenses
♦ Blood: Over the course of the pregnancy, you can expect to be billed anywhere from $100 to $700 for various blood tests.
♦ Ultrasound: At least $200 each. In an ordinary pregnancy, you'll have between none and three.

Prenatal Testing
If you and/or your practitioner decide that you're a candidate for amniocentesis or any other prenatal diagnostic test, you can expect to pay $800–1,200. In most cases genetic counseling is required beforehand, and that costs an additional $300–500. If you're having any prenatal testing done just because you'd like to find out the sex of the baby or want reassurance of its well-being (and not because you're in a high-risk group), your insurance company may not pay for it.

At the Hospital
♦ For a problem-free vaginal delivery and a twenty-four-hour stay, hospital charges will run anywhere from $1,000 to $2,500.
♦ If you're planning to spend the night in the hospital with your partner, hospitals will add about $200 per day extra to your bill.
♦ Anesthesiologists charge from $750 to $1,500 for an epidural, more for a spinal block, even more for a Cesarean section.

If Your Partner Has a Cesarean Section
If your partner requires a C-section, all bets are off. This is major surgery, and it is expensive. The operation, which your OB/GYN will perform, is not included in his or her flat fee, and you'll have to pay for at least two other doctors to assist, plus a pediatrician, who must be in attendance to care for the baby. In addition, a C-section entails a longer recovery period in the hospital—usually four to five days, as well as extra nursing care, pain medication, bandages, and other supplies. If the baby is in good health, he or she may be taken home, but

chances are you will want him or her to stay with your partner, especially if she is breastfeeding. The baby's additional time in the nursery costs more, too. In our case, by the time all the bills had been paid, we (actually, mostly our insurance company) had shelled out more than $15,000 for the birth of our first child. That alone was just about enough to make us decide on a home birth for the second one (although we ultimately opted against it).

An Important (and Possibly Profitable) Word of Advice

Make sure that you and your partner check your birth-related bills *very* carefully. Hospitals can make mistakes, and they are rarely in your favor. After we'd recovered from the shock of the C-section bills (which started off at closer to $17,000), we asked a doctor friend to go over them with us. He found that we'd been charged for a variety of things that didn't happen and overcharged for a lot of the things that did. For example, we'd been billed $25 for a tube of ointment that the hospital's own pharmacy was selling for $1.25. And for the second pregnancy, our nit-picking review of the bills cut about 20 percent off the total.

Now here's the "profitable" part. Since your insurance company will probably be paying for most of your bills, they'll be ecstatic if your review ends up saving them money. In fact, some insurers are so thrilled that they'll actually give you a percentage (sometimes as much as half) of the money they save. Naturally, though, you'll have to ask for your reward. So, read your policy carefully and, if you still have questions, talk to your agent or one of the company's underwriters.

And while you're reading your insurance policy, here are a few other things to look out for:

- **How long before the birth does the insurer need to be notified about the pregnancy and estimated due date?** Not complying with the carrier's instructions could mean a reduction in the amount they'll pay for pregnancy and birth-related expenses.
- **When can the baby be added to the policy?** Until the baby is born, all pregnancy- and birth-related expenses will be charged to your partner. After the birth, however, your partner and the new baby will be getting separate checks (all baby-related expenses, such as medication, pediatrician's exams, diapers, blankets, and various other hospital charges, will be charged to the baby). Some carriers require you to add the baby to your (or your partner's) policy as far in advance as thirty days before the birth; others give you until thirty days after the birth. Again, failing to carefully follow the insurer's instructions could result in a reduction of coverage.

Your Rights to Free and Subsidized Medical Care

♦ Many state health departments operate free health clinics.

♦ Hospital emergency rooms are required by federal law to give you an initial assessment—and any required emergency care—even if you can't afford to pay.

Low-Cost Alternatives

Obstetrical Clinics

If you live in a city where there is a large teaching hospital, you may be able to have your baby at its obstetrical clinic. If so, you'll spend a lot less than you would have for a more traditional hospital birth. The one drawback is that your baby will probably be delivered by an inexperienced doctor or a medical student. This isn't to say that you won't be getting top-quality care. Clinics are often equipped with state-of-the-art equipment and the young professionals who staff them are being taught all the latest methods by some of the best teachers in the country—some of whom will be in the room supervising.

Notes:

Salad Days

What She's Going Through

Physically

♦ Morning sickness (nausea, heartburn, vomiting)
♦ Food cravings—or aversions
♦ Headaches
♦ Fatigue
♦ Breast changes: tenderness, enlargement

Emotionally

♦ Thrilled that she's pregnant
♦ A heightened closeness to you
♦ Apprehension about the nine months ahead
♦ Mood swings and sudden, unexplained crying

What's Going On with the Baby

It's going to be a busy first month. About two hours after you had sex, the egg is fertilized, and after a full day or so there is a tiny bundle of quickly dividing cells. By the end of the month the embryo will be about ¼-inch long and will have a heart (but no brain), as well as arm and leg buds.

What You're Going Through

Thrills

I still have the white bathrobe I was wearing the morning my wife and I found out we were pregnant the first time. I stood nervously in the kitchen, the countertop cluttered with vials of colored powders and liquids, droppers, and the small container filled with my wife's "first morning urine." (Even as

Morning Sickness

About half of all pregnant women experience morning sickness. Despite the name, the nausea, heartburn, and vomiting traditionally associated with morning sickness can strike your partner at any hour of the day. Fortunately, for most women morning sickness disappears after about the third month. Until then, here are a few things you can do to help your partner cope with morning sickness:

♦ Help her maintain a high-protein, high-carbohydrate diet.

♦ Encourage her to drink a lot of fluids—especially milk. You might also want to keep a large water bottle next to the bed. She should avoid caffeine, which tends to be dehydrating.

♦ Be sensitive to the sights and smells that make her queasy—and keep them away from her.

♦ Encourage her to eat a lot of small meals throughout the day, and to eat *before* she starts feeling nauseated. She should try to eat basic foods like rice and yogurt, which are less likely to cause nausea than greasy foods.

♦ Make sure she takes her prenatal vitamins.

♦ Put some pretzels, crackers, or rice cakes by the bed—she'll need something to start and end the day with, and these are low in fat and calories.

♦ Be aware that she needs plenty of rest and encourage her to get it.

recently as 1989, do-it-yourself pregnancy detection kits were a lot more complicated than they are today.) Feeling like a Nobel prize–winning chemist on the edge of making a discovery that would alter the course of the entire world, I carefully dropped several drops of the urine into one of the vials of powder. I stirred the mixture with the specially provided swizzle stick, rinsed it, and slowly added the contents of the other vial.

In all honesty, the results we got twenty minutes later weren't a complete surprise. But that didn't make it any less thrilling. I'd always wanted to have children, and suddenly it seemed that all my dreams were finally going to come true.

Relief . . . and Pride

At the same time, I was filled with an incredible feeling of relief. Secretly, I'd always been afraid that I was sterile and that I'd have to be satisfied with

*"Young kids today don't know how good they have it . . . I remember
the old days before home pregnancy tests."*

taking someone else's kids to the circus or the baseball game. I also felt a
surge of pride. After all, I was a man, a fully functional man—all right, a
stud, even. And by getting my wife pregnant, I'd somehow lived up to my
highest potential.

Irrational Fears

At some point after the initial excitement and sense of relief, a surprising number of men find themselves experiencing an irrational fear that the child their
partner is carrying is not theirs. Psychologist Jerrold Lee Shapiro interviewed
more than two hundred men whose partners were pregnant, and found that
60 percent "acknowledged fleeting thoughts, fantasies, or nagging doubts that
they might not really be the biological father of the child." The majority of these
men don't actually believe their partners are having affairs. Rather, Shapiro
writes, these feelings are symptoms of a common type of insecurity—the fear

many men have that they simply aren't capable of doing anything as incredible as creating life, and that someone more potent must have done the job.

Staying Involved

Exercise

If your partner was already working out regularly before the pregnancy, she won't need any extra encouragement to exercise, and if her doctor approves, she can probably continue her regular physical fitness routine. Some health clubs will ask a pregnant woman to provide a letter from her doctor.

If she wasn't physically active before pregnancy, this isn't the time for her to take up rock climbing. That doesn't mean, however, that she should spend the entire pregnancy on the sofa. Getting sufficient exercise is critical. It will help improve her circulation, thereby ensuring that the baby has an adequate blood supply, and it will keep her energy level high. One way to help her get the exercise she needs is to work out with her. The key is to start easy and not to push her if you see she's feeling tired or winded.

If your budget doesn't permit joining a health club, a pregnancy exercise course is a less expensive alternative. There are also a number of pregnancy workout videotapes on the market.

Workout No-Nos

♦ **High-impact sports** There's a lot of disagreement about whether or not it's possible to induce a miscarriage by falling. Dr. Robert Bradley, who has delivered over 30,000 babies, says that he has "never known a mother to have harmed a baby by any external trauma." Still, most high-impact activities should be avoided.

♦ **Scuba diving and water skiing** Highly pressurized water can be squeezed through the vagina and cervix into the uterus.

♦ **Skiing** Unless you're an expert, and even then take it easy. My wife skiied when she was seven months pregnant but avoided the most challenging runs where she'd have risked a fall.

♦ **Hot tubs/steam baths/saunas** Research indicates that raising a pregnant woman's body temperature by more than two degrees could be dangerous to the fetus. To cool itself, the body moves blood away from the internal organs—including the uterus—and toward the skin.

Exercises and Sports to Do Together

♦ Speed walking
♦ Swimming
♦ Noncompetitive tennis
♦ Easy weight lifting
♦ Golf
♦ Yoga
♦ Paddle tennis

Before starting *any* kind of workout program, discuss the details with your practitioner and get his or her approval.

Nutrition

The principles of good nutrition haven't changed all that much since you learned about the four basic food groups (or, if you're younger, the pyramid of food) in sixth grade. But now that she's pregnant, your partner will need about 300 more calories a day than before. (Of course, if she was underweight before the pregnancy or is pregnant with twins, she might need a little more.)

If she was overweight before getting pregnant, this is *not* the time to go on a diet. At the same time, the fact that she's "eating for two" is *not* a license to eat anything she wants. Your practitioner will undoubtedly suggest a diet for your partner to follow, but here are a few important nutritional basics to keep in mind:

PROTEIN

The average woman needs 45 grams of protein a day, but your pregnant partner should take in 75 to 100 grams per day. When the fetus is eight weeks old, it has about 125,000 brain-cell neurons. By the end of the nineteenth week, there are about 20 billion—the most he or she will *ever* have. Obstetrician F. Rene Van de Carr has found that a high-protein diet—especially during the first nineteen weeks of pregnancy—supports this surge in brain-cell growth in the baby. Lean proteins are always the best bet. Good sources are skinless chicken, lean meats, low-fat cheese, and cooked fish. Eggs (stay away from the raw ones) are another excellent source of protein; hard-boiled, they travel well and make a convenient between-meal snack.

IRON

If your partner doesn't get enough iron, she may become anemic and begin to feel exhausted. Spinach, dried fruits, beef, and legumes are all good sources, but since much of your partner's iron intake is being used to manufacture the fetus's blood, she may need still more. If so, her doctor will prescribe some over-the-counter supplements. If possible, she should take the tablets with a glass of orange juice—it helps the body absorb the iron. One warning: iron supplements frequently cause constipation.

CITRUS (AND OTHER FOODS HIGH IN VITAMIN C)

Vitamin C is critical to the body's manufacture of collagen, the stuff that holds tissue together. It also helps ensure the baby's bone and tooth development. An inadequate level of vitamin C may weaken your partner's uterus, increasing the likelihood of a difficult labor. Your partner should have at least two servings a day of citrus.

CALCIUM

Calcium is critical to the manufacture of the baby's bones. And since so much of your partner's intake of calcium goes directly to the baby, she needs to make sure she's getting enough for herself. The best sources of calcium are milk and other dairy products. But if your partner is allergic to milk, she should stay away from it—especially if she's planning to breastfeed (her milk allergy could be passed to the baby). Good alternate sources of calcium include pink salmon (canned, with soft bones, is okay), tofu (soybean curd), broccoli, calcium-fortified orange juice, eggs, and oyster shell calcium tablets.

GREEN AND YELLOW VEGETABLES

Besides helping form red blood cells, green and yellow vegetables (which, strangely enough, include cantaloupe and mango) are excellent sources of vitamins A and B, which will help your partner's body absorb all that extra protein she'll be eating. Vitamin A may also help prevent bladder and kidney infections. The darker the green, the better it is for your partner. She should try to have a serving or two per day.

GRAINS AND OTHER COMPLEX CARBOHYDRATES

Grains (including breads and cereals) are basically fuel for your partner's body, and she should have at least four servings a day. Since her body will burn the fuel first, if she doesn't get enough there may not be enough for the baby. Grains are generally low in calories and high in zinc, selenium, chromium, and magnesium—all essential nutrients. They're also high in fiber, which will help your partner combat the constipating effect of iron supplements. Good sources includes whole-grain breads (keep her away from white bread for a few months), brown rice, fresh potatoes, peas, and dried beans.

Nutritional and Chemical No-Nos

♦ **Cigarettes** When a mother-to-be inhales cigarette smoke, her womb fills with carbon monoxide, nicotine, tar, and resins that inhibit oxygen and nutrient delivery to the baby. Cigarette smoking increases the risk of low-birth-weight babies and miscarriage.

♦ **Alcohol** Complete abstinence is the safest choice (although your partner's practitioner may sanction a glass of wine once in a while to induce relaxation). One binge, or even just a few drinks at the wrong time (such as when the baby's brain is developing) can cause Fetal Alcohol Syndrome, a set of irreversible mental and physical impairments. And even moderate social drinking has been linked to low-birth-weight babies, learning impairments, and miscarriages in the early stages of pregnancy.

♦ **Fasting** Unless she has the doctor's approval, your partner should *never* go twenty-four hours without eating—especially in the first nineteen weeks of pregnancy, when the baby's brain is developing.

♦ **Over-the-counter or prescription drugs** Consult your doctor before taking *any* medication, including aspirin, ibuprofen, and cold medicines—especially those containing alcohol or codeine.

"Is it organic?"

- **Illegal/recreational drugs** Abstain during pregnancy—unborn children can be born addicted to illegal drugs.
- **Raw meats and fish** These may contain *Toxoplasma gondii*, which can blind the fetus or damage its nervous system. Practitioners do disagree, however, on the magnitude of the risk involved. My wife's first OB/GYN was Japanese; he was not worried about her eating sushi.
- **Cat feces** Although cat feces don't have much to do with nutrition, they do contain high quantities of the same parasite found in some raw meats. So if you have a cat, you should take over the duty of cleaning the litter box for the duration of the pregnancy.
- **Insecticides, weed killers, and the like** Prolonged and repeated exposure to such toxic substances is thought to be linked to birth defects. So, after you change the litter box, do the gardening. And while you're at it, you might as well switch to organic fertilizers and pesticides.
- **Hair dyes** Although no link to birth defects has been proven, the chemical solutions in hair dyes can be absorbed through the scalp into the bloodstream. So it is recommended to avoid dyeing hair during pregnancy. Vegetable dyes are an alternative; they don't last as long, but they look as good as, and in some cases even better and less artificial than, the chemical variety.

WATER

As if she doesn't have enough to do already, your partner should try to drink eight 8-ounce glasses of water a day. This will help her to replace the water she loses when she perspires (something she'll do more during pregnancy), and to carry away waste products.

FATTY FOODS

Your partner will be getting most of the fat she needs in the other things she's eating during the day. And while she'd be better off eating cheese than an order of fries, remember this: a candy bar once in a while probably never hurt anybody.

A WORD ABOUT A VEGETARIAN DIET

If your partner is a vegetarian, there's no reason why she and the baby can't get the nutrition they need—especially if she eats eggs and milk. But if your partner is a strict vegan, you should check with your doctor for special guidance.

A FINAL NOTE ON NUTRITION

Helping your partner eat right is one of the best things you can do to ensure that you'll have a healthy, happy baby (and a healthy, happy partner). But don't be too hard on her—an occasional lapse is not going to cause any serious problems. Finally, be supportive. This means that you should try to eat as healthily as she does. If you absolutely must have a banana split, do it on your own time (and keep it to yourself).

The Hunger Campaign

One of the things I constantly underestimated while my wife was pregnant was how incredibly hungry she would get, and how quickly it would happen. Even though she might have had a snack before leaving the office, by the time she got home she was ravenous.

If you've been doing most of the cooking at your house, things probably won't change much during the pregnancy. But if your partner has been doing most of the cooking, there are a few things you can do to simplify her life a great deal.

♦ **Learn to cook simple, quick meals.** There are plenty of cookbooks specializing in meals that can be made in less than thirty minutes (*The 15-Minute Vegetarian Gourmet* is an example). In addition, most major newspapers run columns featuring easy-to-cook meals using local and

"Why have you brought me here?"

Stocking Up

If you keep the following items on hand you should be able to create a healthy meal or snack any time.

- Unsweetened cereals
- Whole-wheat pasta
- Tomato or vegetable juice
- Whole-grain bread
- Skim milk
- Nonfat cottage cheese
- Low-fat, naturally sweetened yogurt
- Fresh eggs
- Natural peanut butter
- Pure fruit jams
- Bottled water
- Crackers
- Fresh vegetables that can be eaten raw, including carrots, cucumbers, celery, and tomatoes
- Fresh fruit
- Frozen berries and grapes
- Raisins and other dried fruits

seasonal produce. Significantly more expensive alternatives are to stock up on healthy microwavable dinners or order take-out meals.

- **Plan a few meals.** This means you'll have to spend some time reading cookbooks, looking for things that sound good. As you're reading, be sure to write down the ingredients you'll need. Although meal planning doesn't sound all that difficult, it's time-consuming.
- **Do the shopping.** Even if you aren't planning or cooking meals, doing the shopping can spare your partner an hour or so a week of walking around on floors that are tough even on nonpregnant people's feet. In addition, many women who have severe morning sickness find that being in a grocery store, surrounded by so much food, is just too much to stomach. If your partner did the shopping before the pregnancy, ask her to make a *detailed* list of the items she usually bought.
- **Make her a nutritious breakfast shake.** Let her spend a few more precious minutes relaxing in bed in the morning (see page 34 for a good recipe).

Recipes

Power Shake

½ cup skim milk
1 banana
12 strawberries
juice of 2 oranges

Combine ingredients in a blender or food processor and serve over crushed ice or straight up chilled.

Basic Quick Snacks

♦ Peel and slice carrots and celery the night before for your partner to take to work for lunch.

Reading the Small Print

Getting healthy food isn't always as easy as it might seem, and most food manufacturers aren't about to do you any favors. So as you're pushing your cart around the grocery store, be sure to read the labels carefully. In particular, watch out for the following:

♦ **Ingredients** The first ingredient on the list is always the one there's the most of—no matter what you're buying. So, if that healthy ingredient (OAT BRAN!!!) splashed all over the front of the box turns out to be at the bottom of the ingredients list, try something else.
♦ **Sugar—and all the synonyms** Watch out for fructose, corn syrup, corn sweeteners, sucrose, dextrose, and even honey. They're just fancy ways of saying "sugar."
♦ **Words like "drink," "flavored," or "cocktail"** Despite the healthy-looking label, most fruit "drinks" or fruit-"flavored" drinks contain less actual juice than you might guess—often as little as 10 percent, with the rest usually water and sugar.
♦ **Servings** This is one of the most potentially deceptive areas in food labeling. In most cases, the number of calories, grams of fat and protein, and other nutritional information, is given *per serving*. That's all

♦ Boil eggs (for about 10 minutes—get an egg timer) and shell them.

♦ Mix up some GORP (dried fruits, nuts, raisins, sunflower seeds).

Open-Face White Mexican Omelet

3 egg whites

1 teaspoon cilantro, finely chopped

1 small tomato, chopped

¼ cup green and/or red pepper, chopped

¼ cup red onion, diced

black pepper to taste

Separate eggs and discard yolks. Whisk egg whites in a bowl or measuring cup and pour into a medium nonstick frying pan. Turn heat on low. As egg whites begin to cook, add all other ingredients. Simmer until egg becomes firm, and slide omelet onto plate for serving.

very nice, except that manufacturers don't all use the same serving size. For example, I recently saw an 8-ounce package of fairly healthy frozen lasagna. The calories, protein, and fat all seemed okay—until I noticed that the serving size was actually only 6 ounces. This means that since one person would eat the entire 8 ounces, there was really 33 percent more fat and calories than expected.

♦ **Percentage of calories from fat** Most nutritionists agree that pregnant women should keep their percentage of calories from fat to about 30 percent. Manufacturers are now required by law to make this calculation for you. But there's a fairly simple way to figure it out for yourself: just multiply the number of grams of fat by 10. So, if you're buying something that has 100 calories and 5 grams of fat per serving, the percentage of calories from fat is 50 percent (5 grams × 10 = 50).

♦ **A word about additives** When it comes to ingredients, if you can't pronounce it, don't eat it. And while your partner is pregnant, keep her away from saccharine (a popular sweetener), nitrates and nitrites (preservatives commonly found in lunch meats and bacon), and mono-sodium glutamate (MSG—a flavor enhancer especially popular in Asian food). All of these may have negative effects on your unborn child.

Microwave Oatmeal

$\frac{1}{3}$ cup oats (you can use 1-minute, 5-minute, quick, or regular)
$\frac{2}{3}$ cup water
$\frac{1}{2}$ banana, sliced
dash cinnamon
$\frac{1}{8}$ teaspoon vanilla extract
milk
1 tablespoon wheat germ

Put the oats in a 1-quart microwave-safe bowl. Stir in the water, banana, cinnamon, and vanilla. Microwave on high for 2 to 3 minutes, or until the concoction starts steaming or bubbling. Take out and stir again. Add milk to taste. Sprinkle with wheat germ for extra vitamins and protein.

Chocolate Banana Pancakes

$\frac{1}{2}$ cup white flour
$\frac{1}{2}$ cup whole wheat flour
2 teaspoons baking powder
$\frac{1}{4}$ teaspoon cinnamon
pinch salt
$\frac{1}{2}$ tablespoon white sugar
$\frac{1}{2}$ tablespoon brown sugar (if you're missing either kind of sugar,
      just use a whole tablespoon of the one you have)
1 egg
1 teaspoon vanilla extract (optional, but great)
1 tablespoon vegetable oil
a bit less than 1 cup milk
$\frac{1}{2}$ cup chocolate chips
1 tablespoon butter or margarine
3 bananas, sliced

Mix the dry ingredients in a large bowl. Add the egg, vanilla, oil, and milk. Mix into a smooth batter. Add the chocolate chips and mix again. Melt the butter on a heated griddle. Pour the batter onto the griddle in large spoonfuls. Then quickly place several banana slices on each pancake. When the bubbles that form on the surface of the pancakes pop, flip them over. Cook until the second side is as brown as the first, and remove from griddle.

Any of the following salads can be served as a main course for lunch or as a side dish for dinner.

Tomato and Basil Salad

The combination of these 2 ingredients makes a refreshing salad. When available, use fresh basil and local tomatoes for the best flavor.

2 vine-ripened tomatoes
6 to 8 basil leaves
4 tablespoons balsamic vinegar
4 tablespoons extra virgin olive oil
freshly ground black pepper to taste

Slice tomatoes and arrange on serving plate. Shred basil leaves and sprinkle over tomatoes. Cover with the vinegar and oil. Add freshly ground pepper. Cover and refrigerate for at least 1 hour. Remove from refrigerator a half-hour before serving.

Mixed Green Salad with Balsamic Vinaigrette

Combining different types of greens, such as Boston, red leaf, radicchio, arugula, and endive, makes a green salad more interesting. Raw cucumbers, snow peas, French beans, shredded carrots, and cooked beets also add to the flavor, color, and nutrition of a mixed salad. Stay away from croutons, which are high in calories and low in nutrition.

Thoroughly wash and dry greens, place each serving on a flat plate, and arrange whatever selection of vegetables you like on top. Just before serving, pour about three tablespoons of balsamic vinaigrette dressing (see recipe below) over each salad.

BALSAMIC VINAIGRETTE
2 cloves crushed garlic
⅔ cup balsamic vinegar
1 teaspoon Dijon mustard
½ teaspoon chopped parsley
½ teaspoon chopped chives
½ teaspoon chopped basil
⅓ cup oil
salt and pepper

Mix garlic, vinegar, mustard, and herbs together. Whisk oil into the vinegar mixture. Add salt and pepper to taste.

Cucumber Salad

2 large cucumbers, sliced
1 medium Bermuda onion, diced
1 cup cider vinegar
$\frac{1}{2}$ cup nonfat plain yogurt
1 teaspoon fresh dill, chopped

If the cucumbers are not waxy, leave the skin on. Slice the cucumbers thinly
(a food processor does the job best). Combine the diced onion with the
cucumber slices in a large bowl that can be refrigerated. Pour the vinegar and
yogurt over the mixture, cover, and leave in the refrigerator overnight. Serve
cold as a side dish, garnished with the dill.

Low-Calorie Pizza

Create your own combination of toppings, including artichokes, olives, and
squash, and use an assortment of cheeses, such as blue, cheddar, Swiss, and
even low-fat cottage cheese.

4 soft tortillas (found in grocery freezer)
2 fresh plum tomatoes, sliced
3 cloves garlic, minced or crushed
1 cup mushrooms, sliced and sautéed
1 medium onion, chopped and sautéed
6 teaspoons fresh herbs (oregano, thyme, and basil), minced
    (or 3 teaspoons dried)
$\frac{1}{2}$ cup shredded cheese or low-fat cottage cheese

Preheat oven to 350°F. Place tortillas on a lightly greased cookie sheet. Cover
with tomatoes, garlic, mushrooms, onions, and herbs. Add cheese. Bake for
20 minutes or until tortilla is crisp. Serve hot.

Low-Calorie Cream of Zucchini Soup

This recipe can be varied by substituting carrots, potatoes, or celery for zucchini.

3 medium-size zucchini, seeded and cut into $\frac{1}{4}$-inch slices
1 medium white onion, diced
1 small chicken bouillon cube (optional; bouillon cubes usually
    contain MSG)
1 cup nonfat plain yogurt

1 tablespoon fresh dill
salt and pepper

Put zucchini, onion, and bouillon cube in a saucepan. Add just enough water to cover. Bring to a boil and cook until soft (about 10 minutes). Let cool. Transfer to a blender or food processor, add yogurt and dill, and blend until smooth. Add salt and pepper to taste.

Quick and Easy Vegetarian Spaghetti Sauce

2 large onions, chopped
4 tablespoons olive oil
$\frac{1}{2}$ pound mushrooms, thinly sliced
2 16-ounce jars meatless spaghetti sauce
2 14.5-ounce cans stewed tomatoes
1 4-ounce can tomato paste
1 pound tofu, diced into $\frac{1}{2}$-inch cubes
$1\frac{1}{2}$ teaspoons dried basil
generous pinch of cayenne pepper
1 bay leaf
salt and pepper to taste
1 teaspoon sugar
$\frac{1}{2}$ teaspoon garlic powder
1 tablespoon rice vinegar

In a small saucepan, sauté onions in the olive oil over medium heat until they're translucent. Add mushrooms, and sauté for 5 more minutes (until the mushrooms begin to release their liquid). Add all the other ingredients and simmer for 40 minutes. If sauce won't be used immediately, let cool, pour into two-serving containers, and store in freezer. Defrost as needed.

Spa Potato Chips

3 baking potatoes, peeled and thinly sliced
nonstick cooking spray
paprika to taste

Preheat oven to 350°F. Slice potatoes as thinly as possible (a food processor is best). Spray a cookie sheet with nonstick cooking spray. Spread out potatoes evenly in pan. Sprinkle with paprika and bake for about 15 minutes, or until crisp.

Spicy Peanut Butter Pasta

1 pound angel hair pasta
1 tablespoon sesame oil
4 tablespoons peanut or safflower oil
6 cloves garlic, minced
1 generous pinch ($\frac{1}{8}$ teaspoon) red pepper flakes
10 scallions, thinly sliced
$\frac{1}{2}$ cup creamy peanut butter
6 tablespoons rice wine vinegar
6 tablespoons soy sauce
4 teaspoons white sugar
1 cucumber, peeled, seeded, and diced (optional)
cilantro to taste (optional)

Cook pasta according to directions on package. Drain and drizzle with the sesame oil. Set aside. Sauté garlic and pepper flakes in the peanut or safflower oil in a large frying pan. Add scallions. Turn to high heat and stir for one minute. Turn off. Add remaining ingredients and use a wire whisk to thoroughly mix into a thick sauce. Pour over noodles while sauce is still warm. Garnish with cucumber and/or cilantro, if desired.

Garlic Roasted Chicken

1 roasting chicken (3 to 4 pounds)
5 garlic cloves
1 carrot, sliced
2 celery stalks, sliced
4 small white onions
2 teaspoons olive oil
$\frac{1}{2}$ cup white wine (optional)
$\frac{1}{4}$ cup water

Preheat oven to 450°F. Clean chicken and rinse thoroughly with water. Pat dry. Using fingers, make pockets under skin and stuff with garlic cloves. Place chicken in a deep baking dish. Stuff cavity of chicken with carrot and celery slices and onions. Drizzle olive oil on top of chicken. Pour wine and water over chicken. Bake chicken at 450°F for ten minutes to sear. Then reduce heat to 350°F and cook for 30 to 40 minutes, or until the juices run clear when the thigh is pierced with a fork.

Rack of Lamb

A festive, delicious dish that is easy to prepare.

¼ cup bread crumbs
3 cloves garlic, crushed
2 teaspoons parsley flakes
salt and pepper to taste
1 rack of lamb (ask the butcher to crack the rack, remove excess fat, and
    French-cut the ribs)
5 teaspoons Dijon mustard

Preheat oven to 450°F. In a small bowl, mix the bread crumbs, garlic, parsley, and salt and pepper. Place rack of lamb in a baking pan, meat side up. Spread mustard on top and bake for 10 minutes. Remove from oven. Using a fork, press the bread crumb mixture into mustard, reduce heat to 350°F, and cook for about 20 more minutes, or until medium rare.

Fruit Salad with Creamy Yogurt Dressing

A refreshing, low-calorie dish for breakfast, lunch, or dessert. As a side dish or dessert, this recipe serves four. As a main course for lunch, it serves two.

1 green apple, cored and diced
1 banana, sliced
juice of 1 lime
1 small bunch of red or green seedless grapes
5 strawberries, halved
1 seedless navel orange (or other citrus fruit), sectioned
2 kiwis, peeled and sliced
1 cup low-fat vanilla yogurt (or nonfat plain yogurt)
1 teaspoon cinnamon
½ cup shredded coconut (optional)
4 to 8 fresh mint leaves (optional)

In a large mixing bowl combine banana and apple, pour lime juice over them, and mix. Add remaining fruit and mix again. In a separate bowl combine yogurt and cinnamon. Just before serving, mix the yogurt dressing and coconut into the fruit. If fresh mint is available, garnish each serving with one or two leaves.

The Doctor Will See You Now

What She's Going Through

Physically
♦ Continuing fatigue
♦ Continuing morning sickness
♦ Frequent urination
♦ Tingly fingers and toes
♦ Breast tenderness

Emotionally
♦ Continued elation and at the same time some ambivalence about being pregnant
♦ Inability to keep her mind on her work
♦ Fear you won't find her attractive anymore
♦ Continuing moodiness
♦ Fear of an early miscarriage

What's Going On with the Baby

During this month, the baby will change from an embryo to a fetus. By the end of the month, he or she (it's way too early to tell which) will have stubby little arms (no fingers yet), eyes (without eyelids) on the side of the face, ears, and a tiny, beating heart (on the outside of the body). If you bumped into a six-foot-tall version of your baby in a dark alley, you'd run the other way.

What You're Going Through

The Struggle to Connect

Just about every study that's ever been done on the subject has shown that women generally "connect" with their pregnancies sooner than men do. Although they can't feel the baby kicking inside them yet, the physical changes they're experiencing make the pregnancy more "real" for them.

For most men, however, pregnancy at two months is still a pretty abstract concept. For me—as excited as I was—the idea that we were really pregnant was so hard to grasp that I actually forgot about it for several days at a time.

Excitement vs. Fear

But when I remembered we were pregnant, I found myself in the midst of a real conflict—one that would plague me for months. On the one hand, I was still so elated that I could barely contain myself; I had visions of walking with my child on the beach, playing, reading, helping him or her with homework, and I wanted to stop strangers on the street and tell them I was going to be a father. On the other hand, I made a conscious effort to stifle my fantasies and to keep myself from getting attached to the idea of being pregnant. That way, if we had a miscarriage or something else went wrong, I wouldn't be devastated.

Increased or Decreased Sexual Desire

It was during the times when I let myself get excited about becoming a father that I noticed that my wife's and my sex life was changing. Perhaps it was because I was still reveling in the recent confirmation of my masculinity, or perhaps it was because I felt a newer, closer connection to my wife. It may even have been the sense of freedom resulting from not having to worry about birth control. Whatever the reason, sex in the early months of the pregnancy became even more passionate and erotic than before.

But not all men experience an increase in sexual desire during pregnancy. Some are turned off by their partner's changing figure; others are afraid of hurting the baby (a nearly impossible task at this stage of the game). Still others may feel that there's no sense in having sex now that they're pregnant. Whatever your feelings—about sex or anything else for that matter—try to talk them over with your partner. Chances are she's feeling—or soon will be—the same way.

Staying Involved

Going to the OB/GYN Appointments

The general rule that women connect with the pregnancy sooner than men has an exception: men who get involved early on and stay involved until the end have been shown to be as connected with the baby as their partners. And a surefire way to get involved is to go to as many of your partner's OB/GYN appointments as possible.

Going to a doctor wasn't something I ever looked forward to. And going to someone else's doctor was even lower down on the list. But over the course of two pregnancies, I think I missed only two of my wife's medical appointments. Admittedly, some of the time I was bored out of my mind, but overall it was a great opportunity to have my questions answered and to satisfy my curiosity about just what was going on inside my wife's womb.

Theoretically, it's possible to get at least some basic questions answered by reading a couple of the hundreds of pregnancy and childbirth books written for women. But there are other, more important reasons to go to the appointments. First, you will become more of a participant in the pregnancy and less of a spectator. Second, it will demystify the process and make it more tangible. Hearing the baby's heartbeat for the first time (in about the third month), and seeing his or her tiny body squirm on an ultrasound screen (in about the fifth month) bring home the reality of the pregnancy in a way that words on a page just can't do. Third, as the pregnancy progresses, your partner is going to be feeling more and more dependent on you, and she'll need more signs that you'll always be there for her. And while going to her doctor appointments may not seem quite as romantic as a moonlit cruise or a dozen roses, being there with her is an ideal way to tell her you love her and to reassure her that she's not going to be alone.

If you do decide to go to your partner's checkups, you'd better get your calendar out: most women see their health care provider at least once a month for the first seven months, twice in the eighth month, and once a week thereafter. Of course, taking time off from work for all these appointments may not be realistic. But before you write the whole thing off, check with your doctor—many offer early-morning or evening appointments.

Testing

Pregnancy, besides being a time of great emotional closeness between you and your partner, is also a time for medical testing. Most of the tests, such as the monthly urine tests for blood sugar and the quarterly blood tests for other problems, are purely routine. Others, though, are less routine and sometimes can be scary.

The scariest of all are the tests to detect birth defects. One of the things you can expect your partner's doctor to do is take a detailed medical history—from both of you. These medical histories will help the practitioner determine whether or not you are at risk of having a child with severe—or not so severe—problems.

Prenatal Testing

If you are in one of the high-risk categories, your doctor may suggest prenatal testing. You should know that, with the exception of ultrasound and blood tests, each of the other prenatal diagnostic tests involves some potential risks either to your partner or to the baby. Ask your doctor about them and make sure the benefits of taking the test outweigh the potential risks.

ULTRASOUND (SONOGRAM)

This noninvasive test is painless to the mother, safe for the baby, and can be performed any time after the fifth week of pregnancy. By bouncing sound waves around the uterus, the procedure will give you a pretty clear picture of your baby. In the first trimester, your doctor will probably recommend an ultrasound if your partner has experienced any bleeding, if there's any doubt as to the number of fetuses, or if he or she suspects an ectopic pregnancy (a pregnancy that takes place outside the uterus). In the second trimester, you may have an ultrasound to determine the sex of the baby (if you want to), to get a more accurate estimate of the due date, or just because you're curious about what the baby looks like. During the last part of the pregnancy—and especially if the baby is overdue—your partner's doctor may order additional ultrasounds to determine the baby's position, to make sure the placenta is still functioning, or to confirm that there's still enough amniotic fluid left to support the baby.

ALPHA-FETOPROTEIN TESTING (AFP)

This simple blood test is conducted when your partner is 15–18 weeks pregnant. It screens for a variety of neural-tube defects (defects relating to the brain or spinal column), the most common of which are spina bifida and anencephaly (a completely or partially missing brain). The results are available within a week or two. But because AFP is considered quite inaccurate, most obstetricians won't recommend the test unless you or your partner has a family history of neural-tube defects.

OTHER BLOOD TESTS

A variety of genetically transmitted birth defects affect some ethnic groups more than others. So, based on your family histories, your partner's doctor may order one or both of you to get additional blood tests. Among the most common ethnically linked defects are:

♦ Sickle-cell anemia. If you're African American, you should be tested.
♦ Tay-Sachs. If you're both Jewish, and your families are of Eastern European origin, at least one of you should be tested.

AMNIOCENTESIS

This test is usually performed at 15 to 18 weeks, and involves inserting a needle through the abdominal wall into the amniotic sac. A small amount of fluid is collected and analyzed to detect chromosomal and developmental abnormalities. Amnio is extremely accurate and test results are usually available in three to four weeks. Unless your partner is considered at high risk (see page 47) or you want to know everything there is to know about your baby, there's no real reason to have this test. The chances that a woman under thirty will give birth to a baby with a defect that an amnio can detect are less than 1 in 400. The chances that the procedure will cause a miscarriage, however, are 1 in 200. But for a woman over thirty-five, amnio begins to make statistical sense: the chances of having a baby with abnormalities are 1 in 192 and rise steadily as the woman ages.

CHORIONIC VILLI SAMPLING (CVS)

Generally this test is performed at 9 to 11 weeks to detect chromosomal abnormalities and genetically inherited diseases. A catheter is threaded through the vagina and cervix into the uterus, where small pieces of the chorion—a membrane with the identical genetic makeup as the fetus—are snipped off or suctioned into a syringe and analyzed. The risks are slightly higher than with an amnio (the chances of miscarriage are about 1 in 100), but because CVS is potentially much more accurate and can detect a wider range of abnormalities, it is expected to replace amnio in the future.

PERCUTANEOUS UMBILICAL BLOOD SAMPLING (PUBS)

This test is usually conducted at 18 to 36 weeks to confirm possible defects detected through amnio. The procedure is virtually the same as an amnio, except that the needle is inserted into a blood vessel in the umbilical cord; practitioners believe this makes the tests more accurate. Results are avail-

Reasons You Might Be Considered High Risk for Having a Baby with Birth Defects

♦ You or your partner has a family history of birth defects.
♦ You are a member of a high-risk ethnic group (African Americans, for example, are at risk for sickle-cell anemia; Jews of Eastern European descent are considered at high risk for Tay-Sachs).
♦ Your partner is thirty-five or older.

Other Reasons for Prenatal Testing

Prenatal testing is also available to people who, while not considered at risk, have other reasons for wanting it done. Here are some of the most common reasons:

♦ Peace of mind. Having an amniocentesis or a Chorionic Villi Sampling (CVS) test can remove most doubts about the health of your child. For some people, this reassurance can make the pregnancy a much more enjoyable—and less stressful—experience. If the tests do reveal problems, you and your partner will have more time to prepare yourselves for the tough decisions ahead (for more on this, see pages 49–50).
♦ To find out the sex of the baby.

able within about three days. In addition to the risk of complications or miscarriage resulting from the procedure, PUBS also slightly increases the likelihood of premature labor or clotting of the umbilical cord.

Dealing with the Unexpected

For me, pregnancy was like an emotional roller coaster ride. One minute I'd find myself wildly excited and dreaming about the new baby, and the next I was filled with feelings of impending doom. I knew I wanted our babies, but I also knew that if I got too emotionally attached and anything unexpected happened—like an ectopic pregnancy, a miscarriage, or a birth defect—I'd be crushed. So, instead of allowing myself to enjoy the pregnancy fully, I ended up spending a lot of time torturing myself by reading and worrying about the bad things that could happen.

ECTOPIC PREGNANCY

About 1 percent of all embryos don't embed in the uterus but begin to grow in the fallopian tube, which is unable to expand sufficiently to accommodate it. If undiagnosed, an ectopic pregnancy would eventually cause the fallopian tube to burst, resulting in severe bleeding. But the vast majority of ectopic pregnancies are caught and removed by the eighth week of pregnancy—long before they become dangerous.

MISCARRIAGES

The sad fact—especially for pessimists like me—is that miscarriages happen fairly frequently. Some experts estimate that as many as one pregnancy out of five ends in miscarriage. In fact, almost every sexually active woman will have one at some point in her life. (And in most cases the miscarriage occurs before a couple ever knew they were pregnant—whatever there was of the tiny embryo is swept away with the woman's regular menstrual flow.)

Before you start to panic, remember two things: first, over 90 percent of couples who experience a miscarriage get pregnant—and have a baby—later. Second, many people believe that miscarriages—most of which happen within the first three months of the pregnancy—are "a blessing in disguise." The authors of *What to Expect When You're Expecting* sum up this feeling quite well: "Early miscarriage is generally a natural selection process in which a defective embryo or fetus (defective because of environmental factors, such as radiation or drugs; because of poor implantation in the uterus; because of genetic abnormality, maternal infection, random accident, or unknown reasons) is discarded before it has a chance to develop." But if you and your partner have a miscarriage, you probably won't find either of these explanations particularly reassuring.

Until very recently, miscarriage, like the pregnancy it ends, has been considered the exclusive emotional domain of women. This is simply untrue. While men don't have to endure the physical pain or discomfort of a miscarriage, their emotional pain is just as severe as their partner's. They still have the same hopes and dreams about their unborn children, and they still feel a profound sense of grief when those hopes and dreams are dashed. And many men, just like their partners, feel tremendous guilt and inadequacy when a pregnancy ends prematurely.

Some good friends of mine, Philip and Elaine, had a miscarriage several years ago, after about twelve weeks of pregnancy. For both of them, the experience was emotionally devastating, and for months after the miscarriage they were besieged by sympathetic friends and relatives—many of whom had found out about the pregnancy only after it had so abruptly ended. They asked how Elaine was feeling, offered to visit her, expressed their sympathy, and often shared their own miscarriage stories. But no one—not even his wife—ever asked Philip what *he* was feeling, or expressed any sympathy for what *he* was going through, or offered *him* a shoulder to cry on.

Psychologists and sociologists have conducted many studies on how people grieve at the loss of a fetus. But the vast majority of these studies have dealt only with women's reactions. The ones that have included fathers' feelings generally conclude that men and women grieve in different ways. Dr. Kristen Goldbach found that "women are more likely to express their grief openly, while men tend to be much less expressive, frequently coping with their grief in a more stoical manner." This doesn't mean that men don't express their grief at all. Instead, it simply highlights the fact that in our society men, like my friend Philip, have virtually no opportunity to express their feelings.

BIRTH DEFECTS

If one of the tests discussed earlier in this chapter indicates that your baby will be born deformed or with any kind of serious disorder, you and your partner have some serious discussions ahead of you. There are two basic options for dealing with birth defects in an unborn child: keep the baby or terminate the pregnancy. Fortunately, you and your partner won't have to make either of these decisions on your own; every hospital that administers diagnostic tests has specially trained genetic counselors who will help you sort through the options.

When a pregnancy ends unexpectedly or prematurely, it's critical that you and your partner seek out the emotional support you are entitled to. While there's nothing that can be done to prepare for or prevent a miscarriage, telling your partner how you feel—either alone or with a member of the clergy, a therapist, or a close friend—is very important. And don't just sit back and wait for her to tell you what *she's* feeling. Take the initiative—be supportive and ask a lot of questions.

If you're considering terminating the pregnancy for genetic reasons, remember that communicating clearly and effectively with your partner is probably the most important thing you can do during this stressful time. The decision you make should not be taken lightly—it's a choice that will last a lifetime—and you and your partner must fully agree before proceeding with either option.

Don't feel that the two of you have to handle your grief by yourselves: counseling and support are available to both women *and* men who have lost a fetus through miscarriage or genetic termination. Going to a support group can be a particularly important experience for men—especially those who aren't getting the support they need from their friends and families. Many men who attend support groups report that until they joined the group, no one had ever asked how they felt about their loss. The group setting can also give men the chance to stop being strong for their partners for a few minutes and grieve for themselves.

If you'd like to find a support group, your doctor or the genetic counselors can refer you to the closest one—or the one that might be most sympathetic to men's concerns.

Some men, however, are not at all interested in getting together with a large group of people who have little in common but tragedy. If you feel this way, be sure to explain your feelings tactfully to your partner—she may feel quite strongly that you should be there with her and might feel rejected if you aren't. If you ultimately decide not to join a support group, don't try to handle things alone—talk to your partner, your doctor, your cleric, or a sympathetic friend. Keeping your grief bottled up will only hinder the healing process.

Notes:

Spreading the Word

What She's Going Through

Physically
♦ Fatigue, morning sickness, breast tenderness, and other early pregnancy symptoms beginning to disappear
♦ Continuing moodiness
♦ Thickening waistline

Emotionally
♦ Heightened sense of reality about the pregnancy from hearing the baby's heartbeat
♦ Continuing ambivalence about the pregnancy
♦ Frustration and/or excitement over thickening of waistline
♦ Turning inward—beginning to focus on what's happening inside her
♦ Beginning to bond with the baby

What's Going On with the Baby

By now, the little fetus looks pretty much like a real person—except that he or she (an ultrasound technician might be able to tell you which) is only about two or three inches long and weighs less than an ounce. Teeth, fingernails, toenails, and hair are developing nicely, and the brain is not far behind. By the end of this month, the baby will be able to curl its toes, turn its head, and even frown.

What You're Going Through

A Heightened Sense of Reality

During the third month, the pregnancy begins to feel a little more tangible. By far the biggest reality booster for me was hearing the baby's heartbeat, even though it didn't sound anything like a real heart at all (more like a fast hoosh-hoosh-hoosh). Somehow, having the doctor tell us that what we were hearing was really a heartbeat—and a healthy one at that—was mighty reassuring.

Feeling Left Out

While becoming more aware of the reality of the pregnancy is certainly a good thing, it's not the only thing that you'll be feeling at around this point in the pregnancy. Toward the end of this first trimester, your partner will probably begin to spend a lot of time concentrating on what's happening inside her body, wondering whether she'll be a good enough mother, and establishing a bond with the baby. She also may start internalizing her feelings about these processes and may become a little self-absorbed. And if she has a close relationship with her mother, the two of them may develop a deeper bond as your partner tries to find good role models.

Everything she's going through at this point is completely normal. The danger, however, is that while your partner is turning inward or bonding with her own mother, *you* may end up feeling left out, rejected, or even pushed out of the way. This can be particularly painful. But no matter how much it hurts, you should resist the urge to "retaliate" by withdrawing yourself. Be as comforting as you can be, and let her know—in a nonconfrontational way— how you're feeling (see the "Your Relationship" section, pages 60–63). Fortunately, this period of turning inward won't last forever.

Excluded—or Welcomed—by Your Partner's Doctors

For some men—especially those who are feeling left out by their partners— the joy they experience at the increasing reality of the pregnancy is outweighed by the bitterness they feel at the way they're treated by their partner's doctors. Researcher Pamela Jordan found that most men felt that their presence at the prenatal visits was perceived as "cute" or "novel," and that their partners were considered the only patients. If they were talked to at all, it was only to discuss how they could support their partners. The fact that they had needs and concerns didn't seem to occur to anyone.

Fortunately, this was not my experience at all. During both pregnancies, my wife's OBs went out of their way to include me in the process. They made a special point of looking at me when talking about what was happening with my wife and the baby, encouraged me to ask questions, and answered them thoroughly. Our first OB even invited me to take a look at my wife's cervix. I was a little put off by the idea, but getting to see the cervix—through which our baby would emerge just six months later—somehow made the pregnancy seem less mysterious and made me feel much more a part of the whole thing. If your OB doesn't offer you a look, ask for one—I highly recommend it. But be sure to ask your partner first.

Physical Symptoms: Couvade

Although most of what you'll be going through during your pregnancy will be psychological, don't be surprised if you start developing some *physical* symptoms as well. Various studies estimate that anywhere from 22 to 79 percent of expectant American fathers experience *couvade* syndrome (from the French word meaning "to hatch"), or "sympathetic pregnancy." Couvade symptoms are typically the same as those traditionally associated with pregnant women —weight gain, nausea, mood swings, food cravings—as well as some *not* associated with pregnant women: headaches, toothaches, itching, and cysts. Symptoms—if you're going to have them at all—usually appear in about the third month of pregnancy, decrease for a few months, then pick up again in the month or two before the baby is born. In almost every case, though, the symptoms "mysteriously" disappear at the birth.

Considering that our society generally denies the importance (if not the very existence) of what expectant fathers go through during pregnancy, it's not surprising that some men express their concerns and feelings by developing physical symptoms. Among the most common reasons an expectant father might develop couvade symptoms are:

SYMPATHY OR FEELINGS OF GUILT FOR WHAT THE WOMAN IS GOING THROUGH

Men have traditionally been socialized to bite the bullet when it comes to pain and discomfort. And when our loved ones are suffering and we can't do anything to stop it, our natural (and slightly irrational) instinct is to try to take their pain away—to make it *ours* instead of *theirs*. The father of a good friend of mine, for example, had splitting headaches for the last month of all three of his pregnancies.

"Just as your wife suspected, Mr. Sanders. You have a very little boy growing inside you."

JEALOUSY

There's no question that your partner is going to be getting a lot more attention during the pregnancy than you are. And a lot of men who develop couvade symptoms do so in a subconscious attempt to shift the focus of the pregnancy to themselves. My father, who was pacing the waiting room while my mother was in labor with me, suddenly got a gushing nosebleed. Within seconds the delivery room was empty—except for my mother—as three nurses and two doctors raced out to take care of my poor, bleeding father. I'm sure he didn't do it on purpose, but for one brief moment during the delivery, Dad was the complete center of attention.

A LITTLE HISTORY

Most researchers today agree that in Western societies couvade symptoms appear unconsciously in those expectant fathers who experience them. But as far back as 60 B.C.E. (and continuing today in many non-Western societies), couvade has been used *deliberately* in rituals designed to keep fathers involved in the experience of pregnancy and childbirth. Not all these rituals, however, have been particularly friendly to women. W. R. Dawson writes that in the first century mothers were routinely ignored during childbirth, while their husbands were waited on in bed. And more recently, in Spain and else-where, mothers frequently gave birth in the fields where they worked. They then returned home to care for the baby's father.

But in some other cultures, men tried to do the same thing they try to do today: take their partner's pain away by attracting it to themselves. In France and Germany, for example, pregnant women were given their husband's clothes during labor in the belief that doing so would transfer the wives' pains to their husbands. The eighteenth-century Scots believed that a nurse could use witchcraft to transfer the pain of childbirth from the wife to the husband.

Perhaps the most interesting aspect of ritual couvade is the importance attached to the supernatural bond between the father and the unborn child. Whatever the fathers did during the pregnancy was believed to have a direct impact on the unborn child. In Borneo expectant fathers ate nothing but rice and salt—a diet said to keep a new baby's stomach from swelling. In other countries a man who hammered a nail while his wife was pregnant was said to be dooming her to a long, painful labor, and if he split wood, he would surely have a child with a cleft lip. Afraid of making his own child blind, an expectant father wouldn't eat meat from an animal who gave birth to blind young. He also avoided turtles—to make sure that his child would not be born deaf and anencephalic (with a cone-shaped head).

While it's pretty doubtful that couvade rituals actually reduced any woman's childbirth pains or prevented any deformities, they do illustrate an important point: men have been trying to get—and stay—involved in pregnancy and childbirth for thousands of years. As Bronislav Malinowski noted in his 1927 book, *Sex and Repression in Savage Society:*

> Even the apparently absurd idea of couvade presents to us a deep meaning and a necessary function. It is of high biological value for the human family to consist of both father and mother; if the traditional customs and rules are there to establish a social situation of close moral proximity between father and child, if all such customs aim at drawing a man's attention to his offspring, then the couvade which makes man simulate the birth-pangs and illness of maternity is of great value and provides the necessary stimu-lus and expression for paternal tendencies. The couvade and all the cus-toms of its type serve to accentuate the principal of legitimacy, the child's need of a father.

Staying Involved

Spilling the Beans

Another thing (this month anyway) that will make the pregnancy more real is getting to tell people. By the end of the third month, I'd pretty well gotten over my fears of miscarriage or other pregnancy disaster and we'd decided it was safe to spill the beans to our family and close friends. Somehow just saying the words "My wife's pregnant" (I switched to "We're pregnant" a while later) helped me realize it was true.

The decision about when to let other people in on your pregnancy is a big one. Some people are superstitious and opt to put off making the announcement for as long as possible. Others rush to the phone as soon as they get out of bed. Even if you're in the first category, sooner or later you're going to have to start spreading the word—and the end of the third month is a pretty good time.

Whom you decide to tell, and in what order, is your own business. But there are a few guidelines you might want to keep in mind.

FAMILY

Unless you have some compelling reason not to, you should probably tell your family first. Your close friends will forgive you if they hear about the pregnancy from your Aunt Ida; if it happens the other way around, Aunt Ida may take real offense. There are a few cases, however, when telling your family first might not be a great idea. One couple we know, Lawrence and Beth, kept their pregnancy a secret from their friends for five months—and from their family for longer—hoping that Lawrence's brother and sister-in-law, who had been trying to get pregnant for years, would succeed in the interim.

FRIENDS

If you do decide to tell your friends first, make sure you swear them to secrecy—good news travels a lot faster than you might think. As in the case of relatives, be considerate of friends who have been trying but who haven't been as successful as you.

THE OFFICE

You'll probably want to tell your coworkers and your boss (if you have one) at about the same time as you tell your friends. But you should remember that society has some pretty rigid work/family rules for men, so be prepared for a less-than-enthusiastic response from some people (see the "Work and Family" section, pages 88–93, for a complete discussion). Whatever you do,

Trying to Keep the Secret

Despite your attempts to control the flow of information, if you're not careful about what you do, people—especially your close friends—are going to guess. If you're serious about not wanting anyone to know, here are a couple things to keep in mind:

- **Stay away from expressions like "in her condition" or "I think she really needs to rest."** That's exactly how I inadvertently leaked the news to a friend who had asked how we liked working out on the Stairmaster machine at the gym.
- **Be unobtrusive if you change your habits.** If your partner used to drink or smoke before she got pregnant, you might want to think a little about how your friends and family will react to her new, vice-free life-style. When my wife was pregnant with our second daughter, we agreed to meet some good friends at a bar one Saturday night. No one really noticed that my wife was drinking mineral water instead of her usual beer. But when she ordered an ice cold glass of milk, the jig was up.

though, don't wait until the last minute to tell the folks at work—especially if you're planning to take some time off or to make any work schedule changes after the birth.

YOUR OTHER CHILDREN

If you have other children, give them plenty of time to adjust to the news. But do *not* tell them until after you want everyone else to know. Until they're over six, kids don't understand the concept of "keeping a secret." One of our four-year-old's big thrills in life is to whisper in people's ears things that are supposed to be secrets.

You should also make a special effort to include your other children as much as possible in the pregnancy experience. Our older daughter came with us to most of the doctor appointments and got to hold the doppler (through which you hear the fetus's heartbeats) and help the doctor measure my wife's growing belly. Finally, keep in mind that it's perfectly normal for expectant siblings to insist that they, too, are pregnant—just like Mommy. Insisting that they're not may make them feel excluded and resentful of the new baby. This is *especially* true for little boys.

ANNOUNCING YOU'RE PREGNANT

J. GREER

◆ ◆ ◆

No matter how or when you do it, telling people you're expecting will open a floodgate of congratulations and advice; after a few weeks, you may wonder what anyone used to talk about at parties before. Just about everybody has something to say about what you should and shouldn't do now that you're pregnant. You'll hear delightful stories, horror stories, and just plain boring stories about pregnancy and childbirth. You'll probably also have to endure endless "jokes" about your masculinity, speculation about who the "real" father is, and questions about what the mailman or the milkman looks like— mostly, unfortunately, from other men. With attitudes like these, is it any wonder that 60 percent of men have at least fleeting doubts as to the true paternity of their children?

Immediately after breaking the news to our friends and family, my wife and

What If You're Not Married?

Even in the last few years of the twentieth century, when it's the norm
for couples to live together before getting married, having a child out
of wedlock still raises a lot of eyebrows. Your most liberal-minded
friends and relatives might surprise you by suggesting that you "make
an honest woman of her" before the baby comes. Try to keep your
sense of humor about these things. You and your partner are grown-
ups and capable of making the decisions you think best. And anyway, most unmarried parents-to-be find that their relatives' joy at
the prospect of a new little niece, nephew, or grandchild frequently
overshadows those same relatives' disappointment over your lack of a
marriage certificate.

I began to feel some slight changes in our relationship with them. What had
once been our private secret was now public knowledge, and just about everyone wanted to share it with us. People would "drop in" unannounced, usually
bearing either gifts or advice—just to "see how things were going"—and the
phone never stopped ringing.

After a few days, you and your partner may start to feel a little claustropho-
bic. If this happens, don't hesitate to establish some ground rules. For example, you might want to ask your friends and families to call before coming over,
or you might set up—and let everyone know about—specific visiting hours.

You should also prepare yourself for the possibility that you may feel a
little left out. Most people are going to be asking how your partner is feeling,
what she's going through, and so on. Few, if any, will ask the same questions
of you. If you start feeling that you're being treated more like a spectator than
a participant in the pregnancy, there are three basic solutions. First, you can
just ignore the whole thing—no one's deliberately trying to exclude you; it
just doesn't occur to most people that pregnancy, at least at this stage, affects
men all that much. Second, you can sulk. This (although sometimes satisfy-
ing) will probably not get you the kind of attention you're craving. Third, you
can take a proactive role and volunteer information about how the pregnancy
is affecting you. Tell people about how excited you are; confide your hopes
and fears to your friends—especially those who already have kids and can
offer advice. If you're lucky, they'll then start asking you for updates.

*"You're entirely too touchy. My saving grace
is my ability to laugh at myself."*

Your Relationship

COMMUNICATING WITH EACH OTHER

Pregnancy is not only a time of great joy and anticipation, it's also a time of great stress. And even though you and your partner are both pregnant at the same time, you're not experiencing the pregnancy in exactly the same way or at the same pace. This can lead to an increasing number of misunderstandings and conflicts between you and your partner.

As Dr. Shapiro writes, when a couple becomes a family, "generally all the things that are good get better, and all the things that are bad get worse." As your pregnancy continues, then, it's critical to learn to talk—and listen—to each other, and to find ways to help each other through this marvelous, but emotionally bumpy, experience.

As men, we've been conditioned to try to protect our partners from harm. And when our partners are pregnant, protecting them may include trying to minimize the levels of stress in their lives. One way men do this is by not talking about their own concerns. Researchers Carolyn and Philip Cowan write that men fear that mentioning their own worries may not only cause stress to their partners but also expose their own vulnerability at a time when they're expected to be strong for their wives.

The Cowans also found that this overprotective, macho attitude has some very negative side effects. First, because we never give ourselves the chance to talk about our fears, we never learn that what we're going through is normal and healthy. Second, our partners never get the chance to find out that we understand and share *their* feelings.

DANGEROUS ASSUMPTIONS

When I was in the Marines, one of my drill instructor's favorite comments was "Never assume anything. 'Assuming' makes an **ass** out of **u** and **me**." The sergeant's spelling problems notwithstanding (he also thought habitual thieves were called hypochondriacs and that Italians ate bisgetti), he was right about the dangers of making assumptions.

Here are a few important things you may have assumed were no problem. Not all these issues are important to everybody, but if you haven't discussed them already, do it now.

♦ **Your involvement in the pregnancy** Dr. Katharyn Antle May has found that there are three basic styles of father involvement during pregnancy. The *Observer Father* maintains a certain emotional distance and sees himself largely as a bystander; the *Expressive Father* is emotionally very involved and sees himself as a full partner; the *Instrumental Father* sees himself as the manager of the pregnancy and may feel a need to plan

*"Me carrying the baby and you having the cravings
is not my idea of shared responsibility!"*

every medical appointment, every meal, and every trip to the gym. Whatever your style is, make sure to talk it over with your partner. After all,
she's pregnant, too.

+ **Your involvement in family tasks** How much child care are you planning to do when the baby comes? How much is your partner expecting
you to do? How much are you expecting her to do? Several studies have
shown that to some extent, women control their partners' involvement at
home. If a woman wants her partner to take an active role in child care,
he generally wants the same thing. But if she wants to keep these activities to herself, he usually expects to be less involved. In addition, the
Cowans have found that men who take a more active role in running their
households and rearing their children "tend to feel better about themselves and about their family relationships than men who are less
involved in family work."

+ **Religion** Both you and your partner may never have given a thought to
the religious education—if any—you plan to give your child. If you have
thought about it, make sure you're both still thinking along the same
lines. If you haven't, this might be a good time to start.

+ **Discipline styles** How do you feel about spanking your children? Never?
Sometimes? How does she feel about it? How you were raised and whether
your parents spanked you will have a great deal to do with how you raise
your own children.

+ **Sleeping arrangements** It's never too early to give some thought to
where you want the baby to sleep: In your bed? In a bassinet next to you?
In a separate room?

+ **Work and child-care expectations** Is your partner planning to take
some time off after the birth before going back to work? How long? Would
you like to be able to take some more time off? How long? What types of
child-care arrangements do you and she envision?

+ **Finances** Do you need two paychecks to pay the mortgage? If you can
get by on one, whose will it be?

And throughout the pregnancy, don't forget:

+ **Your feelings—good, bad, or indifferent** Talk about your excitement about having a child, your dreams, your plans for the future, your
fears, worries, and ambivalence, and how satisfied you are with your
level of involvement during the pregnancy. But don't forget to ask your
partner what she's feeling about the same things. Have these discussions

regularly—what you and your partner are thinking and feeling in the third month may be completely different from what you'll be thinking and feeling in the fourth, sixth, or ninth months. As difficult as it may seem, learning to communicate with each other now will help you for years to come.

Getting Time Alone

There may be times when you find the pressures of the pregnancy so overwhelming that you need just to get away from it for a while. If so, take advantage of the fact that you don't have a baby inside you, and take some time off. Go someplace quiet where you can collect your thoughts or do something that will give you a break from the endless conversations about pregnant women and babies. Before you go, though, be sure to let your partner know your plan of escape. And whatever you do, don't rub it in: she'd probably give anything to be able to take a breather from the pregnancy for a couple hours.

Here are a few things you might want to do with your free time:
◆ Hang out with some childless friends.
◆ Start a journal about what you're feeling and thinking during the pregnancy.
◆ Go to the batting cages and let off a little steam.
◆ Go for a long drive or for a walk on the beach or in the woods.
◆ Be a kid for a while—blow some quarters on a video game.

Notes:

Money, Money, Money

What She's Going Through

Physically
♦ Nipples darkening
♦ Increasing appetite as morning sickness begins to wane
♦ Clumsy—dropping and spilling things
♦ She may be able to feel some slight movements (although she probably won't associate them with the baby unless she's already had a child)

Emotionally
♦ Great excitement when she sees the sonogram
♦ Worries about miscarriage are beginning to fade
♦ Concerned about what it really means to be a mother
♦ Continuing forgetfulness and mood swings
♦ Increasingly dependent on you— needs to know you'll be there for her, that you still love her

What's Going On with the Baby

During this month, the baby will grow to about four inches long. His or her heart will finish developing and will start pounding away at 120–160 beats per minute—about twice as fast as yours. The baby can now tell when your partner is eating sweet things or sour things. He or she can also react to light and dark—if you shine a strong light on your partner's abdomen, the baby will turn away.

J. OATOR

What You're Going Through

Increasing Sense of the Pregnancy's Reality

By the time the fourth month rolls around, most men are still in what Dr. Kathryn May calls the "moratorium phase" of pregnancy—intellectually we know she's pregnant, but we still don't have any "real" confirmation. Oh, sure, there was the pregnancy test, the blood test, the doctor's pelvic exams, her swelling belly and breasts, the food cravings, and hearing the baby's heartbeat a month before, but even with all that, I had the lingering suspicion that the whole thing was an elaborate, Mission: Impossible–style fake.

But the day my wife and I went in for the ultrasound, everything began to change. Somehow, seeing the baby's tiny heart pumping and watching those bandy little arms and legs squirm convinced me that we might really be pregnant after all.

Can We Really Afford This?

Besides being fun, seeing the ultrasound filled me with a wonderful sense of relief. After counting all the fingers and toes (not an easy task, considering how small they were and how fast they were moving), I felt I could finally stop worrying about whether our baby would be all right.

But my newfound sense of ease didn't last long. I suddenly became possessed by the idea that we couldn't possibly afford to have a baby—not an uncommon thought among expectant fathers.

American society values men's *financial* contribution to their families much more than it does their *emotional* contribution. And expressing strong feelings, anxiety, or even fear is not what men are expected to do—especially when their wives are pregnant. So, as the pregnancy progresses, most expectant fathers fall back on the more traditionally masculine way of expressing their concern for the well-being of their wives and little fetuses: they worry about money.

Some men express their financial worries by becoming obsessed with their jobs, their salaries, the size of their homes, even the rise and fall of interest rates. Expectant fathers frequently work overtime or take on a second job; others may become tempted by lottery tickets or get-rich-quick schemes. Insurance agents and financial advisors sometimes try to take advantage of an expectant father's concerns about money by encouraging him to buy insurance policies he doesn't need or make investments he and his family can't afford. Clearly, a new baby (and the decrease in household income while the mother is off work) can have a significant impact on the family's finances. But as real as they are, write Libby Lee and Arthur D. Colman, authors of *Pregnancy: The Psychological Experience,* men's financial worries "often get out of proportion to the actual needs of the family. They become the focus because they are something the man can be expected to handle. The activity may hide deeper worry about competence and security."

Safety—Your Partner's and the Baby's

As if worrying about finances weren't enough, many expectant fathers find themselves preoccupied with the physical health of the other members of their growing family (but not their own—studies have shown that men go to the doctor much less frequently than usual when their partners are pregnant).

I'd seen the ultrasound and knew that the baby was fine. And I'd already read that at this point in the pregnancy, there was very little chance of a miscarriage. But still, I worried. I quizzed my wife about how much protein she was eating; I reminded her to go to the gym for her workouts; I even worried about the position she slept in. (Sleeping on the back is a bad idea; the baby-filled uterus presses on the intestines, back, and a major vein—the inferior vena cava—and could cause hemorrhoids or even cut off the flow of oxygen or blood to both your partner and the fetus.) All in all, I was a real pain.

A word of advice: If you're feeling overly concerned and protective of your partner and your baby, be gentle and try to relax a little. Your partner probably has the same safety concerns you do. If you're still worried, discuss your concerns with her practitioner at your next appointment.

Staying Involved

Focus on Her

Although every pregnant woman will need and appreciate different things, there is a lot more common ground than you might imagine. Basically, she

Ways to Show Her You Care

Here are some ideas that will make you popular around the house (and make your wife the envy of all of her friends—pregnant and otherwise):

◆ Offer to give her back rubs and foot massages.

◆ Suggest activities that might be harder to do when the baby comes, like going to movies or concerts.

◆ Bring home roses for no reason at all.

◆ Vacuum the house—even under the bed—without being asked.

◆ Give your wife lots of hugs; research shows that the more she is hugged, the more she will hug the baby.

◆ Buy her a moisturizing bubble bath.

◆ If you're traveling on business, arrange to have a friend take her to dinner.

◆ Offer to pick up a pizza on your way home from work—and surprise her with a pint of her favorite frozen yogurt, too.

◆ Offer to run errands (pick up cleaning, shop, go to the drug store, and so forth).

◆ Do the laundry before it piles up.

◆ Tell her you think she's going to be a great mother.

◆ If she arrives home after you, have a candlelight dinner on the table, complete with sparkling cider.

◆ Write her a love letter and send it to her in the mail.

◆ Buy a toy or outfit for the baby, have it gift-wrapped, and let her unwrap it.

- Buy her a pretty maternity dress.
- Go on a long walk with her.
- Learn baby CPR.
- Offer to give her a back rub—again.
- If you smoke, stop.
- Tell her she's beautiful.
- Pay extra attention to making sure she has enough to eat—pack some snacks for her before the two of you go out for an evening or for a hike.
- Keep a list of your favorite names or buy her an interesting name book.
- Paint a picture for or write a letter to your unborn baby.
- Offer to set up interviews with potential child-care people.
- Buy her a Mother's Day gift.
- Keep a journal (either written, tape-recorded, or videotaped) of what you're thinking and feeling during the pregnancy.
- Subscribe to parenting magazines.
- Take her to visit the nursery at your local hospital.
- Help her address envelopes for the birth announcements.
- Learn easy recipes (see pages 34–41).
- Invite her to go swimming somewhere beautiful.
- If you already have children, take them to the park and let your partner have time alone to relax or run an errand she's had to put off.
- Surprise her with breakfast in bed on a lazy Sunday. Or, on a workday, get up five minutes earlier and surprise her with a power shake.
- Give other expectant mothers seats on trains and buses.
- Make a donation to a children's hospital.
- Make a donation to a school.
- Discuss your fears with your wife and listen to hers. Be certain not to belittle her fears—no matter how small they may seem to you.
- Paint or wallpaper the baby's room.
- Help put together the changing table and crib.
- Install smoke detectors in your house.
- Make a new will that includes your baby.
- Join a health club together.
- Clean out closets to make room for baby things.
- Call her on the phone during the day—just to tell her you love her.
- Offer to carry her bags.
- Buy a few tapes of her favorite music to listen to in the labor room.

needs three things from you now—and for the rest of the pregnancy—more than ever before: expressions of affection, admiration, and support (both verbal and physical) for *her;* sensitivity to her changing physical condition (hunger, fatigue, muscle pains, and so on); and expressions of affection and excitement about the *baby* and your impending parenthood.

Finances

PLANNING A COLLEGE FUND

It may seem hard to imagine now, but in eighteen years or so the baby you haven't even met yet is going to be graduating from high school and heading off to college. And so, at the risk of reinforcing the old stereotype that a father's role in his children's lives is primarily financial, it's time to talk about money.

From the mid-1970s to the mid-1990s, college tuition and expenses, such as room and board, rose about 5 to 8 percent a year. Experts project that these costs will continue to rise by about 6 to 7 percent a year. This means that by the year 2015 a *single year* at a public college will cost more than $36,000; at a private college, costs will exceed $77,000.

If you're not independently wealthy, this may sound like an exorbitant amount of money—especially when you consider that you'll have to come up

"I just found out what braces cost."

with the same amount four years in a row. But if you establish a well-thought-out college fund now, things won't be as bad as you think. And if you're lucky, you might even be able to afford to have another kid.

Within the scope of this book it would be impossible to cover the full range of educational investment possibilities. So we've chosen to focus on a few of the most common alternatives. After you've considered what we have to say, we recommend that you get yourself a stockbroker or a financial planner and make sure that the education fund you're considering fits in with your overall financial objectives. But be wary of those who recommend that you do all of your investing through them. You should also have your accountant take a look at what you're planning.

ZERO COUPON BONDS are bonds issued by the U.S. Government and by corporations that you purchase for a small fraction of what they'll be worth when they mature (face value). You could, for example, pay $200 today for a bond that would be worth $1,000 by the time your child enters college. The price you pay now, and what the bonds will be worth at maturity, depend on current interest rates (the higher they are, the less you pay now) and when they mature (the longer you hold them, the less you pay).

The advantages of zeros are:
- You can pick any maturity date, from next year to thirty years in the future.
- You can lock in current interest rates until maturity.
- You know exactly what they'll be worth when they mature.
- There's an active market for zeros. So if you have a financial emergency, you can sell the bonds for whatever they're worth at that time.
- With government-issued zeros there's absolutely no risk of default.

The disadvantages of zeros are:
- You can't take advantage of changes in interest rates (if rates rise after you've bought a bond, you're out of luck).
- Even though you don't actually receive any money until the bond matures, you have to pay taxes on the interest earned each year. (You can, however avoid this problem by buying tax-exempt zero coupon municipal bonds.)
- If you don't hold the bonds to maturity, you may lose some of your principal.

SERIES EE SAVINGS BONDS are a type of zero coupon bond issued by the U.S. Government that, like zero coupon bonds, you purchase at a fraction of their face value.

The advantages of EE bonds are:
- Unlike zeros, they pay an adjustable rate of interest (a guaranteed 85 percent of the average market yield on five-year Treasury securities) if you hold them at least five years.
- No taxes are due until the bonds are cashed. This means you get to keep more of the interest you earn, which means that you get more interest on your interest, which means that you'll have more money at maturity.
- They may be *entirely* tax-free if you cash them in only for your child's education.

The disadvantages of EE bonds are:
- You can invest a maximum of $15,000 per year in EE bonds.
- Unlike zeros, there's no market for these bonds. All you can do is cash them in. You won't have to pay a commission, however.
- If you and your partner earn over $60,000 combined (the IRS will adjust this amount every year for inflation), the "entirely tax-free" advantage noted above doesn't fully apply.

PREPAID TUITION PLANS Some states have plans that allow you to prepay all or part of your child's state college tuition costs. How much you pay depends on when you expect your child to start college, and on current interest rates. Some private colleges offer similar programs.

The advantages of prepaid tuition plans are:
- These plans usually offer good value for the money.
- Tuition is fully paid.

The disadvantages of these plans are:
- If your child doesn't end up going to the college you selected eighteen years before, all you'll get back is the principal you put in—the interest you would have earned will be lost.
- You may have to pay taxes on the difference between what you pay today and what tuition costs eighteen years from now.

MUTUAL FUNDS save you the trouble of trying to put together your own stock or bond investment program. There are more than four thousand different mutual funds available—ranging from high-risk to low-risk—enabling you to pick the one that most closely matches your needs. Over the past ten years, mutual funds have increased an average of about 13 percent a year—significantly more than the rate of inflation.

HOW OFTEN TO INVEST

If you have the money, the best way to finance your child's college education is to invest an amount equal to four years of today's private-school tuition and fees right now. As the cost of education goes up, so will the value of your investment. Thus, by the time your child reaches college age, the entire cost of his or her education will be covered.

If you don't have the money now, you should invest as much as you feel you can afford, as often as you can afford to. The best way to do this is through a system called "dollar cost averaging." This means that on a regular basis—weekly, monthly, quarterly—you contribute a fixed amount to the same mutual fund or other investment. When prices are up you're buying fewer shares; when prices are down, you're buying more. A stockbroker friend says that dollar cost averaging is by far the best overall long-term investment strategy.

The problem with this or any other regular savings plan is remembering to do it. If things get tight—as they have plenty of times at my house—the education checks can get "overlooked" or "rescheduled." Fortunately, most brokerage houses allow you to have your specified investment automatically deducted from your checking or savings account, effectively creating a forced savings plan.

A NOTE ON TAXES

Whatever investment program you're considering, remember one thing: put it in your child's name. The first $500 of income earned by a child under fourteen is tax-free each year. The next $500 is taxed at 15 percent, which is probably less than your tax rate. Income over $1,000 a year is taxed at your rate.

What this means is that as soon as your child's investment account begins to earn over $1,000 a year, you ought to consider putting any future investments into tax-free zeros or mutual funds. That way, the tax liability will be kept to a minimum. Another option is to invest in aggressive-growth funds that will bring in the highest returns, and pay the taxes you'll owe along the way.

One final note: before you can start an investment program in your child's name, you'll have to have his or her Social Security number, which means you'll have to wait until he or she is born. So take advantage of the next few months and spend some time talking over with your partner what your educational objectives are, how much you have to invest, how much risk you're willing to tolerate, and how many children you're planning to have.

INSURANCE

LIFE INSURANCE While you may not think that this is the time to be talking about life insurance, you couldn't be more wrong. Because there are so many different kinds of life insurance, and because each of them is right only in certain circumstances, we're not going to go into much detail here. Suffice it to say that you and your partner should get life insurance if you don't have any, or meet with your agent to discuss if and how your new baby will change your insurance needs. The point is that if, God forbid, either of you dies unexpectedly, the survivor shouldn't have to worry about having to get a better job just to keep up the mortgage or private-school tuition payments.

LIFE INSURANCE FOR CHILDREN This one is pretty simple. In most cases, taking out a life insurance policy on a child is a complete waste of money. The one exception is if you're getting a policy that builds cash value.

Choosing a Financial Planner, a Stockbroker, or an Insurance Broker

- ♦ The safest way to start your search for a representative is to ask trusted friends and family members for their recommendations.
- ♦ Every family is different. You need a representative who's willing to take the time to get to know you and your goals for the future. You also need someone who is willing to answer every question you have, no matter how basic.
- ♦ Check the person out. This means asking for personal and professional references and following up on them. Some highfalutin-sounding certifications are nothing more than alphabet soup and mean only that the person paid a few hundred bucks to join an organization.
- ♦ Things change fast. So get together with your representative to review your overall financial plan once a year.

But if your aim is to build cash value, you'd probably get a higher return by putting the money into a mutual fund or other investment.

DISABILITY As long as you've got insurance on your mind, you really should take a long, hard look at disability coverage. If your employer offers a long-term disability policy, sign up now. If not, explore the subject of getting one of your own through your broker. In many cases, a long-term disability could be more devastating to your family's finances than death.

GETTING PROFESSIONAL ADVICE

Over the course of the next twenty years or so, you're probably going to be spending a lot of your hard-earned money on health, life, and disability insurance; college investment plans; and retirement plans. The way you spend all that money will have a powerful—and long-lasting—effect on you and your family. So, unless you're a financial planner, stockbroker, or insurance agent yourself, you've probably got no business making major financial decisions without advice. The problem, of course, is how to get the best advice (see page 73).

Notes:

The Lights Are On and Somebody's Home

What She's Going Through

Physically

♦ Can feel the baby's movements—
  and she knows what they are
♦ May have occasional painless
  tightening of the uterus (Braxton-
  Hicks contractions)
♦ Continuing darkening of nipples,
  appearance of dark line from belly
  button down the abdomen

Emotionally

♦ Very reassured by the baby's
  movements and less worried
  about miscarriage
♦ Developing feeling of bonding
  with the baby
♦ Sensitivity about her changing
  figure
♦ Increase in sexual desire
♦ Increasingly dependent on you
♦ Feelings of jealousy (after all,
  it was her private pregnancy
  until now)

What's Going On with the Baby

The baby can now close his or her eyes and is beginning to grow eyelashes
and hair on the head. He or she is about nine inches long and kicks, punches,
grabs at the umbilical cord, and can even suck his or her thumb. Best of all,
he or she can now hear what's going on outside the womb.

What You're Going Through

Oh My God, I'm Going to Be a Father

I have to admit that even after seeing the baby on the sonogram, I still found it hard to believe I was really going to be a father (the technology to fake a sonogram must exist, right?). But when my wife grabbed my hand, placed it on her belly, and I felt that first gentle kick, I knew the whole thing was true. And as usual, after the initial excitement passed, I found something to worry about.

More Interested in Fatherhood

After that first kick, I suddenly became consumed with the idea that I just wasn't ready to be a father. I still wanted children—nothing had changed there—but I suddenly realized that in only four months I would face the biggest challenge of my life, and I didn't know a thing about what I was getting into. I felt as though I were about to attempt a triple back flip from a trapeze—without a safety net.

I had already done a lot of reading about pregnancy and childbirth, but I felt I still didn't know what fathers really *do*. Doesn't it seem a little strange—scary, really—that you need to have years of training and take loads of tests before you can get most jobs, but there are absolutely no prerequisites for the far more important job of being a father?

Feeling the baby's first kicks may make you much more interested in reading about pregnancy, if you haven't been doing so already. You may also find yourself wanting to spend more time with friends or relatives who have small kids or just watching how other men interact with their children.

Turning Inward

You've had a lot to think about lately—your family's finances, your new role as a father, your partner's (and your baby's) safety. So don't be surprised if you begin to become preoccupied with your own thoughts—sometimes to the exclusion of just about everything else, even your partner.

Although this sort of "turning inward" is perfectly normal, make every effort to keep from distancing yourself from your partner. If you can, tell her what's on your mind; it'll probably make you feel a lot better. (If you're having a tough time opening up, you might want to review the "Your Relationship" section on pages 60–63.)

At the same time, though, remember that she may be feeling insecure and need to be reassured that you aren't going to leave her. She may also be feeling emotionally needy and crave confirmation of your love for her. Pay close attention to her subtle (or not so subtle) hints and make sure she gets the attention she needs. If she doesn't, she may think you don't care. As Arthur and Libby Colman write, "A man who ignores his partner's anxieties may find they escalate rather than abate with a condescending 'Everything is going to be all right, dear.'"

Staying Involved

Prenatal Communication

As we've discussed elsewhere, good communication is a critical part of your pregnancy. But what about communicating with your unborn child? While the very idea may sound a little wacky, research has shown that months before they are born, fetuses are extremely responsive to what's happening "on the outside."

For your partner, communicating with your unborn child is quite a bit different—or at least more convenient—than it is for you. After all, she and the fetus are physically connected; and she can talk to it, sing to it, or rub it through her belly any time of day or night. But just because your access to the baby is comparatively limited doesn't mean you can't communicate with it.

There's no question that unborn babies can hear. In one study, an obstetrician inserted a microphone into a woman's uterus while she was in labor (after her water had broken), and recorded the external sounds that could be heard from the inside. He got clear recordings—not only of voices and the mother's internal body sounds but also of Beethoven's Ninth Symphony, which was being played in the delivery room.

Hearing is one thing, but are babies actually affected by what they hear from within the womb? Absolutely. Researcher Anthony DeCasper asked sixteen women to make a tape of themselves reading a poem called "The King, the Mice, and the Cheese," and two different tapes of Dr. Seuss's *The Cat in the Hat*. Then, during the last six and a half weeks of their pregnancies, the women were instructed to choose only one of the stories they'd recorded (roughly a third of the women chose each story) and play it three times a day for their unborn child.

When the babies were three days old, DeCasper offered them a choice between the story they'd heard over and over or one of the other stories. Since three-day-old babies aren't real good about speaking up, DeCasper used a "suck-o-meter" (a specially rigged pacifier that enabled the babies

---

**A Few Things to Remember about
Prenatal Communication**

♦ Respect your partner. You've got a right to speak with your child, but she's got a right to privacy.
♦ Try to overcome the feeling that what you are doing is absolutely ridiculous.
♦ Don't whisper. Speak to the fetus loudly enough so that a person standing across the room could hear you clearly.
♦ Don't do it when you're feeling bored. The fetus will pick up on your tone of voice.
♦ Don't get your expectations too high. There's very little you or anyone else can do to guarantee that your child will be a genius.
♦ Have fun.

---

to determine which story they'd get to hear merely by changing their sucking speed) to allow the children to express their preferences. Fifteen out of the sixteen babies chose the story they'd heard while in the womb. If nothing else, this research ought to convince you that even before they're born, babies' lights are on and there's somebody home.

So why should *you* try to communicate with your growing fetus? First of all, because it's kind of fun. In the evening, I used to place my hands on my wife's belly and tell the current resident all about what I'd done during the day. Sometimes I'd even do "counting" exercises with them: I'd poke once and say (loudly), "One." Most of the time, I'd get an immediate kick back. A few seconds later, I'd poke twice and say, "Two." Frequently, I'd get two kicks back.

The second reason to try some prenatal conversations is that they can help you establish a bond with your baby before the birth. It may even help make the pregnancy seem a little more "real." I've got to admit that in the beginning, the idea of talking to a lump in my wife's belly seemed silly. But after a while I got used to it and began to feel a real closeness with the baby. Another father felt that by communicating extensively with his unborn daughter, he was able to establish a loving relationship with her while she was still inside. And when she finally was born, he described their first meeting as "like meeting someone face to face with whom you had only spoken on the telephone."

In addition, communicating with your unborn child will help him or her develop a bond with *you*. Many fathers are jealous of the immediate bond newborn children have with their mothers. It seems, though, that this bond may have more to do with the mother's voice (which the baby has heard every day for nine months) than anything else. Dr. DeCasper, in another suck-o-meter study, found that nine out of ten newborns selected a story recorded by their own mother over the same story recorded by another woman. By getting your baby used to your voice, he or she will be able to begin bonding with you immediately.

A third reason to try prenatal communication is that there's some evidence that you can influence the type of person your child turns out to be. Boris Brott (yes, he's a relative, but I've never met him), a famous Canadian orchestra conductor, traces his interest in music to the womb:

As a young man, I was mystified by this ability I had to play certain pieces sight unseen. I'd be conducting a score for the first time and, suddenly, the cello line would jump out at me: I'd know the flow of the piece before I turned the page of the score. One day, I mentioned this to my mother, who is a professional cellist. I thought she'd be intrigued because it was always the cello line that was so distinct in my mind. She was; but when she heard what the pieces were, the mystery quickly solved itself. All the scores I knew sight unseen were ones she had played when she was pregnant with me.

In an effort to harness the power of prenatal communication, several physicians and obstetricians have developed organized communication systems. Psychiatrist Thomas Verny says that by singing and talking to the fetus, "parents create a positive intrauterine environment, reducing the level of anxiety-producing hormones that lead to frenetic activity and even ulcers in the unborn." Going one step further, Dr. Rene Van de Carr says that his program, the Prenatal Classroom, provides systematic stimulation that may "actually help the growing fetus' brain become more efficient and increase learning capacity after birth." Perhaps the most fantastic claims, though, are made by psychiatrist Brent Logan. Logan, who uses what he calls the "cardiac curriculum" to pump a set of increasingly complex heartbeatlike sounds into the mother's womb, says his "graduates" frequently learn to talk as early as at five or six months and to read at eighteen months (most kids don't usually talk until they're at least a year old, or read until they're five or six).

For more information about prenatal learning, I recommend reading Rene Van de Carr's and Thomas Verny's books, both of which may be available in your local public library (see bibliography).

Sex

Pregnancy can do funny things to your libido. Some expectant fathers are more interested in sex and more easily aroused than ever before. Others are repelled by the very idea. Whether you're feeling either of these ways or something in between, rest assured that it's completely normal.

In this section, we'll talk about the sexual issues that may come up in the first six months of your pregnancy. Late-pregnancy sexual issues are covered on pages 114–15.

WHY YOU AND /OR YOUR PARTNER MIGHT BE FEELING *INCREASED* SEXUAL DESIRE

- After about the third month, her nausea and fatigue are probably gone, making sex more appealing.
- You may find her pregnant body (with its larger breasts and fuller curves) erotic.
- Your partner may be proud of her more ample figure and may be feeling sexier.
- You may be turned on by the feeling of power and masculinity at having created life.
- Your partner may be turned on by the confirmation of her femininity and by the awe at what her body is doing.
- Throughout pregnancy, you both may experience a newfound feeling of closeness that frequently manifests itself sexually.

WHY YOU AND /OR YOUR PARTNER MIGHT BE FEELING *DECREASED* SEXUAL DESIRE

- In the first trimester, your partner may be too nauseated or tired to be interested in sex. In the second trimester, she may feel too uncomfortable or too awkward to want to have sex (about 25 percent of pregnant women feel this way).
- She may think that you don't find her attractive and don't want to have sex with her.
- You may *not*, in fact, be attracted to a woman whose body has been transformed from fun to functional.
- You may think your partner isn't feeling attractive and wouldn't be interested in sex.
- You or your partner may be afraid that sex will hurt her—or the baby. In fact, there's nothing to be afraid of. The baby is safely cushioned by its amniotic fluid–filled sac, and, unless your doctor feels there are exten-

uating circumstances, sex during pregnancy is no more dangerous for your partner than at any other time. You (and your partner) may find this information reassuring. If you do, great; if not, now may be the time to talk about and try some different sexual positions (lying on your sides or with your partner on top, for example) and different ways of bringing each other to orgasm (oral sex, vibrators, and so on). Often simply making a few such changes can go a long way toward alleviating your fears.

♦ Although in most cases sex is required to become a parent, you and your partner may feel, as it gradually sinks in that you are about to become parents, that parents aren't supposed to be sexual. (Even though we are all living proof that our parents had sex at least once, it's somehow hard to imagine the two of them, in bed, naked . . .)

♦ You or your partner may feel that sex serves only one purpose: creating children. And once you've done that, there's no more need for sex—until you want more kids.

WHAT THE EXPERTS SAY

As you can see, the range of feelings about sex is broad. But if you still aren't convinced that you're not the only one feeling the way you do, here are a few interesting things researchers have found out about expectant couples' sexuality during pregnancy:

♦ According to psychologists Wendy Miller and Steven Friedman, expectant fathers generally underestimate how attractive their partners feel, and expectant mothers consistently underestimate how attractive their partners find them. (The bottom line is that most men find their pregnant partners' bodies erotic, and most pregnant women feel quite attractive.)

♦ According to the Cowans, expectant fathers have more psychological inhibitions about physical intimacy during pregnancy than their partners do.

♦ The old myth that pregnancy somehow desexualizes women is just that— a myth. In fact, Miller and Friedman found that there are no significant differences in the level of sexual desire or sexual satisfaction between expectant men and women.

WHEN YOU AND YOUR PARTNER ARE OUT OF SYNC

Of course, you and your partner may not always be on the same wavelength. She may feel like having sex just when you're feeling put off by her Rubenesque figure. Conversely, you may want to have sex at a time when she's simply not interested. Here are a few suggestions that might help:

♦ **Talk.** At these and so many other times during your pregnancy, communicating with your partner is essential. As Arthur and Libby Colman so wisely write, "Unless the couple can talk about their sex life, their entire relationship may suffer, and that in turn will compound their sexual problems."

♦ **Try some nonsexual affection,** such as snuggling, touching, or just hugging each other. And say up front that that is what you're interested in doing, because it isn't as easy as it sounds. Professors Cowan and Cowan have found that many couples need practice finding sensual ways to please each other short of intercourse. And both men and women hesitate to make affectionate overtures if they aren't sure they're ready to progress to intercourse and are worried they'll be misinterpreted.

♦ **Be nice to each other.** Being critical of her figure will make her feel self-conscious, less attractive, and less interested in sex.

Notes:

Work and Family

What She's Going Through

Physically
♦ Period of greatest weight gain begins
♦ Increased sweating
♦ Increased blood supply gives her that pregnant "glow"
♦ Increased fetal activity

Emotionally
♦ Moodiness is decreasing
♦ Continued forgetfulness
♦ Feeling that the pregnancy will never end
♦ Increased bonding with the baby
♦ Still very dependent on you

What's Going On with the Baby

The baby is now covered with vernix, a thick, waxy protective coating. The movements of the now foot-long two-pounder are getting stronger, and he or she can hear, and respond to, sounds from outside the uterus.

What You're Going Through

Reexamining Your Relationship with Your Father
As the reality of your prospective fatherhood unfolds, you'll probably find yourself spending a lot of time contemplating how you'll reconcile the various roles—parent, provider, husband, employee, friend—that will make up your paternal identity. As mentioned in earlier chapters, you may be spending more time reading about childhood and watching how your male friends, or even strangers, juggle these roles.

But eventually you'll realize that your own father—whether you know it or not—has already had a profound influence on the kind of father you'll be. You also may find yourself nearly overcome with forgotten images of childhood—especially ones involving your father. Just walking down the street, I'd suddenly remember the times we went camping or to the ballet, how he taught me to throw a baseball in the park, and the hot summer afternoon he, my sisters, and I stripped down to our underwear in the backyard and painted each other with watercolors. There's nothing like impending paternity to bring back all the memories and emotions of what it was like to be fathered as a child.

Not all childhood memories of fathers are positive. Many men's images of their fathers are dominated by fear, pain, loneliness, or longing. Either way, don't be surprised if you find yourself seriously reexamining your relationship with your father. Was he the kind of man you'll want to use as your role model? Was he the perfect example of the kind of father you *don't* want to be like? Or was he somewhere in between? Many men, particularly those who had rocky, or nonexistent, relationships with their fathers, find that the prospect of becoming a father themselves enables them to let go of some of the anger they've felt for so long.

Don't be surprised if you start having a lot of dreams about your father. Dream researcher Luis Zayas found that an expectant father's uncertainty about his identity as father, his actual role, and the changed relationship with his wife and family are "among the psychic threads of fatherhood" that are fundamentally related to the man's relationship with his own father and are frequently present in his dreams.

So, whether you're awake or asleep, as you're thinking about your father, remember that what's really going on is that you're worried about what kind of a father *you* will be when your baby arrives.

A Sense of Mortality

Although I've always been more than just a little fascinated by death, it wasn't until my wife got pregnant the first time that death became more than a mere abstraction. Suddenly it occurred to me that my death could have a serious impact on other people.

This realization had some interesting and fairly immediate results. The first thing that happened was that I became a much better driver—or at least a safer one. Overnight, yellow lights changed their meaning from "floor it" to "proceed with caution." I began to leave for appointments a few minutes earlier so I wouldn't have to hurry, I wove in and out of traffic less, and I found myself not quite so annoyed with people who cut me off in traffic. But besides becoming a better driver, I began to look back with horror at some of the risky things—parachuting, scuba diving—I'd done before I'd gotten married, and I began to reconsider some of the things I'd tentatively planned for the near future—bungee jumping, hang gliding. After all, now there were people counting on me to stay alive.

My preoccupation with my own mortality had other interesting consequences as well. I found myself strangely drawn to my family's history; I wanted to learn more about our traditions, our history, our family rituals, the wacky relatives no one ever talked about. I even bought a family-tree computer program and began bugging my relatives about their birth dates. Apparently it's quite common for expectant fathers to experience a heightened sense of attachment to their relatives—both immediate and distant—even if they weren't particularly close before.

This really isn't so unusual, especially when you consider that one of the main reasons we have kids in the first place is so that a little piece of us will live on long after we're gone. I guess the hope is that one day seventy-five years from now, when my great-grandson is expecting a child, he'll start to explore his roots and want to get to know more about me.

Feeling Trapped

As we've already discussed, you and your partner probably aren't feeling the same things at the same time. Earlier on in the pregnancy, your partner may have turned inward, preoccupied with how the pregnancy was affecting *her.* You may have felt a little (or a lot) left out. By now, though, your partner may be "coming out"—concentrating less on herself and the baby, and more on you.

Meanwhile, you may have just begun the process of turning inward. You're going to be a father in less than four months, and you've got a lot of things to think about, many of which you need to work through on your own. The potential problem here is that just as you begin to focus on yourself, your partner is becoming increasingly dependent on you. She may be afraid that you don't love her anymore and that you're going to leave her. Or she may be worried—just as you are—about your physical safety. Although being doted upon is nice, it can sometimes get out of hand. And your partner's increased dependence on you may cause you to feel trapped. As the Colmans found, a pregnant woman's "sudden concern may make a man feel over-protected, as though his independence is being threatened." If you are feeling trapped, it's important to let your partner know in a gentle, noncon-frontational way. At the same time, encourage her to talk about what she's feeling and what she wants from you.

Staying Involved

Having Fun
Besides being a time of great change—physical as well as emotional—preg-nancy can be a fun time, too. Here are a few ways to amuse yourselves:

- ♦ **Take lots of pictures.** I took regular shots of my wife—from the front and the side, with emphasis on the belly—holding a mug-shot-style card labeled "Pregnant Woman Number 1 (2, 3, and so on)." For another series of photos, she stood up while I lay on my back between her legs and took pictures of her soft underbelly. If you don't have a camera that marks the date right on the prints, you'll want to take note of the critical day the belly completely blocks your view of your partner's face. Take pictures at least once a month until the eighth month, then once a week after that.
- ♦ **Get some special clothes.** His and hers "Yes sir, that's my baby" T-shirts, and "Father-to-bee" hats (featuring a picture of a bumble bee) are favorites.
- ♦ **Get some exercise—together.** Taking a water aerobics or swimming class together can be a lot of fun. You'll be amazed at how agile pregnant women can be when they're floating in water. Unless you're quite confi-dent about your partner's sense of humor, it's best to stifle your comments about whales—beached or otherwise.
- ♦ **Start a clipping file for the baby.** Just before our older daughter was born, my wife started putting together a file with newspaper and magazine photos of the hot fashions of the day; lists of the top ten movies, books, and records of the year; articles on the pressing political and social issues of the day; pictures of the house we live in and the baby's room—before and after we fixed it up; and ads—showing the prices, of course—for a variety of items (houses for sale in our neighborhood, computers, food, movie and theater tickets, and so on).
- ♦ **Go shopping for baby announcements.** Or, you can design your own. See pages 101–2 for more details.

♦ **Make a plaster belly cast.** Believe it or not, this is my all-time favorite. It's a little complicated, but well worth the trouble. Long after the baby is born, you, your partner, and your friends will be absolutely amazed that your partner was ever that big (and the baby that small). If you're interested in trying it, Francine Krause (P.O. Box 1024, Guerneville, CA 95446 [707] 869-3925) sells a wonderful kit that includes all the materials you'll need. An important warning: Don't even *think* about making a cast of your partner's belly using any kind of plastic, rubber, or resin. No matter what anybody tells you, these products can be extremely harmful to both your partner and the baby.

Work and Family

FAMILY LEAVE

Let's face it: for a man, staying involved with the fetus is possible only a few hours a week—a little before work, a bit more after work, on weekends. But what about *after* the pregnancy? Is a few hours a day going to be enough time to spend with your child? If it were, you probably wouldn't be reading this book.

Contrary to the common stereotypes, most fathers want to spend a lot of time with their families. Consider the results of a few recent studies:

♦ One major corporation found that 57 percent of men (up from 37 percent five years earlier) wanted work-schedule flexibility that would enable them to spend more time with their families.

♦ A *Los Angeles Times* poll found that 39 percent of men say they would quit their jobs and stay home with the kids.

♦ Three out of four fathers consider family to be the most important aspect of their lives.

♦ Eighty percent of fathers want to take more of a role in parenting than their own fathers did and expect to make parenting a fifty-fifty proposition with their wives.

Despite contemporary fathers' good intentions, however, only about *1 percent* of men ever take advantage of their companies' family-leave options when they have the chance. So what accounts for the contradiction between what men *say* and what they actually *do*? First of all, the vast majority of family-leave plans (including the recently enacted Family and Medical Leave Act of 1993) are unpaid. Since the average working woman still makes less than the average working man, if one person is going to take time off from work, many families conclude that they can better survive the loss of the woman's salary.

The Family and Medical Leave Act of 1993

The Family and Medical Leave Act of 1993 is not a simple document to understand. You can (and should) get a free copy from your senator or congressional representative. Here's a summary of what it means for fathers:

♦ **Who can take the leave?** Any person who works for a company that employs fifty or more people, has been employed by that company for at least twelve months, *and* has worked at least 1,250 hours.

♦ **How much leave can you take?** Eligible employees can take up to twelve work weeks of leave at any time during the twelve-month period that starts the day your child is born. Be careful, though: if you and your wife are employed by the same company, you are entitled to a *total* of twelve weeks between you.

♦ **Is it paid?** Employers are not required to pay you your salary while you're on leave. But say your employer pays for six weeks of family leave, you're still entitled to take another six without pay.

♦ **What about benefits?** Your employer must maintain your coverage under the company's health plan for the duration of your leave.

♦ **Is your job protected?** In most cases, yes. Your employer cannot fire or replace you while you're on leave unless he or she can prove that your being gone has caused "substantial and grievous economic injury to the operations of the employer."

♦ **Do you have to give notice?** Under the act, you're required to give your employer at least thirty days' notice before taking your family leave. But the more notice you give, the more time everyone will have to get used to the idea.

Check with your state's employment department to see whether it offers family-leave benefits that are more liberal than those of the federal program. In California, for example, companies that employ twenty-five or fewer people are required to offer their employees family leave (as opposed to the federal program's fifty-employee minimum).

Family Leave If You're an Employee

♦ **Take the leave.** Every man I interviewed who took family leave told me he'd do it again. One even told me he thought that men who *didn't* take family leave were "nuts."

♦ **Know your rights.** Find out whether you're eligible for family leave under the Family and Medical Leave Act of 1993 (see page 89), your company's voluntary plan, or any other government- or state-mandated program.

♦ **Start talking to your employer** *now.* If you're covered by a leave plan, start working out the details in a nonthreatening, nonconfrontational way. If you're *not* covered by a leave plan, you may be able to arrange for some time off anyway.

Family Leave If You're an Employer (or Supervisor)

♦ **Take the leave yourself.** The ultimate responsibility for helping men get more involved with their families rests at the top—with male managers. If you set an example and take family leave yourself, everyone else will see that it's okay and follow your lead.

♦ **Encourage other men to take the leave.** Most of your male employees will be reluctant to approach you with their family-leave plan. If you know they're pregnant, raise the issue with them first. Chances are, they'll be grateful. At Los Angeles Water and Power, employee turnover dropped drastically after the Doting Dads program started.

♦ **Don't worry about the cost.** Companies with liberal family-oriented benefits have found that the costs incurred to keep a job open for a man on leave or to redistribute his workload while he's gone are more than made up for in improved morale and increased productivity.

But financial pressure isn't the only reason men don't take family leave. Even when their companies offer *paid* paternity leave (less than 2 percent of all employers), men still don't participate. Why not? A lot of men have a deep-rooted conviction that getting on the "daddy track" will hurt their careers. Tom, an attorney friend of mine who elected not to take advantage of his firm's paid

*"Adorable, Kravitz, but from now on
baby pictures will suffice."*

family-leave plan, told me: "I wanted to take the leave, but I knew I'd never make partner if I did. All the male associates knew it would be career suicide."

Unfortunately, Tom's fears are not unfounded. Dr. Joseph Pleck, of Wellesley College, says that "because employers don't understand or accept the idea of child-care leave for anyone, they find the concept of paternity leave incomprehensible, or simply frivolous." It's not surprising, then, that many companies send their male employees mixed messages about whether or not it's okay to take family leave. A few years before the Family and Medical Leave Act was signed, one major study found that most firms that voluntarily offered gender-neutral family-leave plans didn't advertise that they could be taken by fathers. And when the researchers asked more than 1,500 human resources directors and CEOs how much time they thought would be reasonable for men to take as paternity leave, 63 percent said, "None." Even at companies that did offer paternity leave, 41 percent said *no* amount of paternity leave was reasonable. Sadly, even today, when most larger employers are required by law to grant family leave to men, the prevailing attitude hasn't changed.

Some companies, however, are bucking old conventions; having decided that simply offering paternity leave isn't enough, they're *encouraging* their male employees to take it. For example, in 1991 the Los Angeles Department of Water and Power (78 percent of whose employees are men) started a complete fathering program called Doting Dads. The highly publicized program includes a four-month paternity-leave plan, a father mentorship program, child-care referral services, and even breastfeeding classes for both spouses. Between 1980 and 1990 (before the program started), a total of only three or four men took paternity leave. But after Doting Dads came into being, the number of men taking paternity leave has grown to about thirty each year. A few other large employers have begun to notice a small increase in the number of men who take family leave. The numbers are still minuscule—especially when compared to the number of women who take additional time off after the disability portion of their maternity leave has run out—but it's progress.

LONG-TERM WORK-SCHEDULE CHANGES
So far we've talked about taking a few weeks off just after the birth of your child. But what about after that?

Not long after our first daughter was born, my wife left her big, downtown law firm and found a less stressful, three-day-a-week job closer to home. Almost everyone we knew applauded. But when I made the announcement that I, too, would be cutting back to three days a week, the reaction was quite a bit different. At work, I was hassled repeatedly by my boss and coworkers, and a lot of my friends and relatives began to whisper that if I didn't go back to work full-time, my career might never recover.

For the most part, flexible schedules, job sharing, part-time work, or working-at-home options have been considered "women's issues." But they're not. As a new (or a veteran) father, you're probably going to want to spend more time with your children than your own father did, and just about the only way you'll get to is to make some changes in your work schedule.

I'm not suggesting that everyone should cut back their work schedules to three days a week. Clearly, that just isn't practical for most people (although it sure would be nice, wouldn't it?). But there are a few other ways to increase the amount of time you spend with your family.

JOB SHARING
More and more companies are recognizing that their employees—at least their female ones—need more flexibility than a traditional job can provide. One solution is to have two people share a job—and a desk—at the office. For example, one person might work in the mornings, the other in the afternoons.

WORKING AT HOME (TELECOMMUTING)

While many managers feel they have to see their employees on a daily basis to supervise them, this just isn't the case. Years ago, when I was a commodities trader, I used to spend eight or nine hours a day on the phone haggling with people—most of whom I never met—about grain prices. My coworkers were similarly occupied, and my boss was two thousand miles away. Realistically, there was no reason I couldn't have been working at home.

Granted, commodities trading is not a typical job, but the fact is that many Americans do work that doesn't require their physical presence in any particular place at any particular time. If you're not a construction worker or a retail salesman, you might be a prime candidate for telecommuting.

Now before you start to panic, I'm not suggesting that you rent out your office to someone else—most telecommuters work only a day or two a week at home. The point is that being able to telecommute is just another option that can allow you a little more time with your family. Remember, though, that telecommuting is *not* meant to be a substitute for child care.

If you think you might want to try telecommuting, here's what you'll probably need:

+ a computer (compatible with your employer's system)
+ an additional phone line or two
+ a modem
+ a fax machine (or a send/receive fax/modem)
+ a quiet place to set things up

As great as working at home is, there are still a few disadvantages. Some of my friends began to think that since I was always at home, I wasn't really doing anything, and since I wasn't doing anything, I could run errands for them. If this happens to you, you're going to have to learn to say no. Working at home can also get a little lonely—you might miss hanging out around the water cooler and schmoozing with your buddies at work.

Notes:

Entering the Home Stretch

What She's Going Through

Physically

♦ Increasing general physical discomfort (cramps, dizziness, abdominal achiness, heartburn, and so forth)
♦ Itchy abdomen
♦ Some increased clumsiness
♦ Learning to walk in a new, awkward way
♦ Some thick, white, vaginal discharge (it's called *leukorrhea,* and is completely normal)
♦ Increased Braxton-Hicks (false labor) contractions

Emotionally

♦ Decreased moodiness
♦ Dreaming/fantasizing about the baby
♦ Concerned about work—not sure she'll have the energy to go back, and concerned about how to balance roles of mother, wife, employee . . .
♦ Fear about the labor and delivery

What's Going On with the Baby

The baby's lungs are maturing and he or she can now move in rhythm to music played outside the womb. Weighing in at three pounds and measuring fifteen inches long, he or she is starting to get a bit cramped in the uterus and may spend a lot of his or her free time sucking a thumb.

What You're Going Through

Increasing acceptance of the pregnancy

As we've discussed earlier, for most expectant fathers the process of completely accepting the pregnancy is a long one—with the baby becoming progressively more real over the course of the nine months. "It's like getting the measles," said one man interviewed by researcher Katharyn May. "You get exposed, but it takes a while before you realize that you've got it." Another researcher, Pamela Jordan, found that despite seeing the fetus on a sonogram many men don't really experience their children as real until they meet them face-to-face at birth.

Visualizing the Baby

The growing reality of the pregnancy is reflected in men's dreams as well. Researcher Luis Zayas has found that in expectant fathers' dreams in the early and middle stages of the pregnancy "the child is not represented as a person. Instead, symbols of the child are present." But as the pregnancy

"I want kids. He wants children."

advances to the final stage, expectant fathers—consciously and uncon-sciously—produce clearer images of their children.

If you're discussing this with your partner, keep in mind that women typi-cally begin visualizing their children very early in pregnancy. These visions, which occur both in daydreams and night dreams, undoubtedly have some-thing to do with the physical link the woman has with the fetus, as well as with the fact that many women—thanks largely to socialization—readily view themselves as mothers. In addition, pregnant women generally dream and fan-tasize about *babies*, while their partners imagine themselves with three- to five-year-old children. This was certainly true for me. In almost every dream or fantasy involving children that I had while my wife was pregnant, I was holding hands, leaving footprints on the beach, or playing catch—all things you can't do with an infant. My wife, in contrast, dreamed of a palm-sized, hairless baby who talked to her like an adult.

Speculating about Gender

Like it or not, our society is fixated on gender. So it's not surprising that most parents (if they don't already know) eventually—or constantly—speculate about the sex of their unborn baby. Is your partner carrying the baby high? Wide? Low? Are the baby's kicks hard enough to move your hand, or are they more gentle? Is your partner's complexion clear, or does she have a little acne? There are literally hundreds of absolutely, positively surefire ways of determining what flavor your baby will be—and before your baby is born, you'll hear every one of them.

But before you start believing any of the stories you hear, there are a few things you might find interesting:

 ♦ Most expectant fathers express a preference for boys.
 ♦ Most women claim to have no preference.
 ♦ More women than men call the unborn baby "it." However, both men and women prefer to call the baby by some kind of nickname.

In our case, the nicknames we gave our in-utero daughters stuck with them long after they were born. We called our older "The Roo"—as in kanga—because she kicked so hard she could knock an open book off my wife's belly. And we called our younger "Pokey" because, unlike her sister, she preferred to jab and poke.

If you have a preference for the gender of your child, you might think about keeping it to yourself. If your child turns out to be of the "wrong" gen-der, chances are he or she will eventually find out about it (probably from

CRAWFORD

an unthinking friend or relative whom you once told). The feeling of being inadequate, of "letting you down," and even of being secretly rejected or loved less, may haunt the child for many years, especially in adolescence, when self-confidence is often at a low. So even if you have such a preference in your heart of hearts, there is little to gain—and plenty to lose—by spreading the word.

Some expectant fathers are actually afraid of getting a child of the "wrong" gender, feeling that if they do, they won't be able to have the parenting experience they'd imagined. For many men, their images of themselves as parents are closely linked to the gender of their children. As boys, we spent a great deal of our childhood engaging in physical activities such as running, jumping, wrestling, and playing football. So it's natural to imagine ourselves doing the same things with our own children. Yet some men feel uncomfortable with the idea of wrestling with their daughters, believing that playing physically with girls would somehow be inappropriate. The truth of the matter is that not only is it safe and appropriate to play physically with girls, it may also be quite beneficial for them in some unexpected ways (see pages 185–87 for more on this).

Fear of Falling Apart During Her Labor

Men are supposed to be strong, right? Especially while their wives are pregnant. And any sign of weakness could be taken as an indication of, well, weakness. Perhaps it's those old societal pressures that make most men dread labor—not only because they aren't looking forward to seeing their partners in pain, but because they're afraid that they'll simply fall apart. And everybody knows that real men don't crack under pressure.

If you're worried about how you'll perform during your partner's labor, do yourself two favors:

♦ Read the "Classes" section on pages 102–10—especially the "What If You Feel Like You Don't Want to Be in the Delivery Room at All?" section at the end.

♦ Remember that it rarely happens. Dr. Jerrold Shapiro interviewed more than two hundred expectant fathers, none of whom fell apart during his partner's labor.

Staying Involved

Choosing a Name

Naming a child may sound like an easy task, but it's harder than you think. And you'd better start thinking about it soon, because the second question you're going to hear after the baby comes (the first being "Boy or girl?") is "What's the baby's name?" Here are a few things you might want to keep in mind as you begin your search:

♦ Think about the future. That cute name you're considering if you have a girl might sound pretty ridiculous when she turns out to be a Supreme Court justice.

♦ According to the author of *The Best Baby Name Book in the Whole Wide World,* boys who have peculiar names (Armin, for instance) have a higher incidence of mental problems than boys with common ones, and than girls with peculiar ones.

♦ Do you need—or want—to honor a relative?

♦ Do you want a name that indicates your ethnic or religious background?

♦ Do you want something unique yet manageable?

♦ Do you want something easy to spell and/or pronounce?

♦ How do you feel about the nicknames that go with it?

♦ How does it sound with the last name? How would the nicknames sound with the last name?

♦ No, you can't use numbers. (There was a real-life court case a while back about a guy in Minnesota who tried to change his name to a number. He lost.)

HOW TO PICK 'EM

Start by making a list of the ten boys' and ten girls' names you like best. Exchange lists with your partner and cross off all the ones on her list you

couldn't possibly live with. She'll do the same to your list. If there are any
names left, you're in business. If not, keep repeating the process until you
come up with names acceptable to you both. Some couples who absolutely
cannot agree on two names decide instead to let one partner choose the name
if it's a boy and the other choose the name if it's a girl (and let the loser choose
the next child's name).

Not only is this little exercise fun, but it will also give you and your partner
some interesting insights into each other's minds. My wife, for example, had
never really taken my interest in mythology seriously until the names Odin
(the chief god in Norse legends) and Loki (the Norse god of mischief and evil)
showed up on my top-ten list. I don't know what I'm more grateful for, that
both those choices were vetoed or that both our children are girls.

If you need a little help, here are a few books—each containing thousands
of names and their meanings—you might want to check out:

+ *The Best Baby Name Book in the Whole Wide World,* by Bruce Lansky
  (Meadowbrook, 1984), offers 13,001 possibilities.
+ *Name Your Baby,* edited by Lareina Rule (Bantam, 1986), claims to have
  over 10,000 suggestions.
+ *20,001 Names for Baby,* by Carol McD. Wallace (Avon, 1992).
+ *Proud Heritage,* by Elza Dinwidde-Boyd (Avon, 1994), offers 11,001
  names for African-American babies.
+ *Multicultural Baby Names,* by M. J. Abadie (Longmeadow Press, 1993),
  offers 5,000 African, Arabic, Asian, Hawaiian, Hispanic, Indian, and
  Native American names.
+ *The New Age Baby Name Book,* by Sue Browder (Workman, 1987) has
  10,000 possibilities and is filled with other really great information.
+ *Beyond Jennifer and Jason,* by Linda Rosenkrantz and Pamela Satran
  (St. Martin's Press, 1994). If you're moving to England, pick up *Beyond
  Charles and Diana,* by the same authors (St. Martin's Press, 1992).

It might seem as though these books pretty well cover all the bases, but
out of the 174,003 names my wife and I looked at, we came up with only four
that worked for us (a first and middle for each daughter).

Another approach—albeit an odd one—to picking names is offered by
Albert Mehrabian in his book *The Name Game* (Signet, 1992). Mehrabian
surveyed two thousand people, asking them to judge several thousand first
names and rate them according to success, morality, health, warmth, cheer-
fulness, masculinity/femininity. Not surprisingly, Mehrabian found that certain names evoke certain stereotypes. Bunny, for example, scored high on

femininity, but low on morality and success. Ann and Holly were highly rated in all categories. For boys, Grover and Aldo were big losers in all categories, while Hans (go figure) was rated highly across the board.

So what does all this mean? No one knows. Some onomasticians (people who study names) claim that a child's name has a direct and profound effect on the kind of a life, and successes, he or she will have. Some cite a study in which fifth- and sixth-grade teachers were asked to grade identical essays called "What I Did Last Sunday." The essays "written" by Michael and David were given one full grade higher than those "written" by Elmer and Hubert. Similarly, Karen and Lisa outperformed Bertha by one and a half grades. Other studies have shown that, contrary to popular opinion, unusual names may actually have a *positive* effect for college women.

FAMILY PRESSURES/TRADITIONAL CUSTOMS

In many cultures (or families), your choice of names may be severely limited by tradition.

+ Among the Kikuyu people of Africa, the family's first son is named after the father's father; the second son, after the father's grandfather; the first daughter, after the father's mother; and so on.
+ In Burma, each day of the week is assigned a different letter of the alphabet and children's names must begin with the letter of the day on which they were born.
+ In Thailand, the parents may ask a nearby priest—or even a fortune-teller—to give their child just the right name.
+ Jews of Eastern European extraction generally don't name babies after living people because of the traditional fear that the Angel of Death might take the baby instead of the older namesake.
+ If there is someone on either side of a family who absolutely has to be honored with a name for the sake of family peace, you may be able to find a reasonable compromise. Harry Truman's parents, for example, gave him the middle initial *S*—no name, no period, just the initial—to satisfy both grandfathers (whose names were Solomon and Shippe).

THE LAST-NAME GAME

If you and your partner already have the same last name, you haven't got anything to worry about; if you don't, there could be a few complications.

Perhaps we've lived in Berkeley too long, but my wife and I have various friends who have done all of the following when they had kids:

- Given the kids the man's last name (common enough)
- Given the kids the woman's last name (less common)
- Given the kids a hyphenated last name (but when Benjamin Brandt-Finnell marries Sarah Rosenberg-Wohl, what will *their* children's last name be?)
- Made up a completely new last name
- Given the boys the man's last name, and the girls the woman's

Birth Announcements

WHEN TO ORDER

Since you don't know the exact weight, height, and (in most cases), gender of the baby before he or she is born, there's not much sense in having birth announcements printed until then. But running around trying to decide on birth announcements is about the last thing you're going to want to do after the baby is born. So now is a good time to pick out the kind you want.

There are three basic types of birth announcements: the preprinted kind with blanks for you to fill in; the custom-made variety; and those you design yourself. Fill-in-the-blank and custom-made announcements are available at most stationery and card shops. If you're ordering custom-made announcements, you can select the design you want in advance and then call in the baby's vital statistics as soon as you know them. Whatever type you choose, try to get the envelopes now and address them while your lives are still relatively calm.

WHAT TO INCLUDE

As medical science becomes more exact, birth announcements will probably contain your baby's IQ and future profession. But for now, most standard birth announcements include the baby's name, date and time of birth, weight, length (since they can't stand up, babies don't usually have "height"), and the names of the parents.

WHOM TO SEND ANNOUNCEMENTS TO

Family and friends are the obvious recipients. When it comes to more casual acquaintances and business associates, however, exercise restraint. Many people will feel obligated to send a gift if they receive a birth announcement, so don't send one to anyone from whom you wouldn't feel comfortable getting a gift. Exceptions include people who request an announcement as a memento,

Baby Showers

Not too long ago, baby showers—like so many other baby-related activities—used to be considered "for women only." But today, if your partner's relatives or friends organize a shower for her, there's a good chance you'll be invited, too. (It's still pretty unlikely that your friends or relatives will plan one especially for you.)

The vast majority of baby showers take place several weeks or months before the baby is born, and the idea behind them is obvious: give the new parents a selection of baby clothing, furniture, and toys so the soon-to-be newborn can come home to a well-stocked nursery. If your relatives and friends are so inclined, enjoy—a shower can be a wonderful way to share your excitement about the coming event with others. And don't forget to keep track of who gave what—after the birth, when you get around to those thank-you notes, all those yellow sleepers can look disconcertingly similar.

For some, however, the idea of having a baby shower before there's a baby seems kind of creepy—after all, what if, God forbid, something were to happen to the baby? If you fall into the anti-shower camp, you may find that some people might be offended by your not wanting one. In such cases, you might want to steer them toward a post-birth shower instead (call it a "Welcome Baby" or "Baby Birthday" party if you want to stay away from the word "shower"). Be firm. Stressing how much more fun it will be for the guests to get presents for a baby whose name and gender are known may also make the no-shower news easier to swallow.

employers or employees who have already given you and/or your partner a baby gift and/or shower, and people your parents and in-laws ask you to send announcements to.

Classes

Until the late 1960s, there really was no such thing as childbirth education. Basically, all you had to know to have a baby was where the hospital was located. And all that expectant parents did to prepare for the arrival of their baby was set up a nursery. Women checked into the hospital, labored alone in stark, sterile rooms, received general anesthesia, and woke up groggy and tender, not even knowing the sex of the child they'd delivered. Meanwhile, men were left to pace anxiously in hospital waiting rooms until a nurse came to give them the happy news. Fathers who tried to buck their nonrole in the birth of their children were in for a real surprise. Dr. Robert Bradley, in *Husband-Coached Childbirth,* cites the 1965 case of a man who was arrested and fined for having "gained unauthorized admission to a hospital's delivery room in an attempt to witness the birth of his second child."

Today, however, the situation is radically different. It's hard to find a man who didn't already, or isn't planning to, attend the birth of his children (according to recent statistics, 90 percent of fathers-to-be are present at the birth) and just about everyone involved in the process—from parents to doctors—has given the word *preparation* a whole new meaning. Mothers and fathers frequently attend prenatal OB/GYN visits together, and many embark on a reading program reminiscent of cramming for college exams. In addition, an increasing number of expectant couples are signing up for childbirth preparation classes. When my wife and I got pregnant for the first time, one of the first things we did was read everything we could get our hands on. By the time the baby was born, we'd probably read enough magazine and newspaper articles, books, and pamphlets to qualify for a degree in prenatal education. But unlike my various "real" degrees, which were fairly useless once I got out into the real world, my education in childbirth and child raising has served me quite well.

SELECTING A BIRTHING CLASS

When the first childbirth preparation classes appeared in the late 1960s, the emphasis was on how to have a natural, unmedicated childbirth. Recently, however, the focus has changed somewhat. While natural childbirth is still the goal of most classes today, the overriding principle is that the more you learn about pregnancy and the birth process—from good nutrition and exercise to the types of pain medications most frequently given to laboring women—the less you have to fear and the more in control you'll feel.

Most classes are taught in groups and give you an opportunity to ask questions about the pregnancy in a less hurried environment than your practitioner's office. They also allow you to socialize a little with other pregnant couples and compare notes. But, depending on the class and the other couples, you may not get as much out of the socializing part as your wife does. When my wife and I took our birthing classes, for example, the teacher lectured most of the time; the socializing consisted of the women discussing how much weight they'd gained, how painful their backs were, and how many times a night they had to get up to go to the bathroom. What was helpful for me was the class itself. And by the time we'd finished, I felt that whatever

happened, whether we had a "natural" birth or a medicated one, whether my wife had a C-section or an episiotomy (an incision to enlarge the vaginal opening), I'd know what was happening at every stage and what to do.

What distinguishes one childbirth method from another is the approach each takes to relaxation and coping with pain. Here's a little about the most common methods:

LAMAZE On a trip to Russia, Dr. Ferdinand Lamaze learned of an approach to pain called *psychoprophylaxis*, which held that pain was a learned reflex and that if a woman were given something else to focus on, her pain would be relieved. The Lamaze method uses the woman's breathing patterns as the object of focus. In addition, Dr. Lamaze incorporated extensive education in anatomy and physiology in the belief that the more a mother knew, the more she could concentrate on what was happening instead of on the pain she was feeling.

BRADLEY Instead of trying to distract the woman's attention from her pain, Dr. Robert Bradley believes that she should just "go with it." If she feels like groaning, she's encouraged to groan; if she feels like screaming, she's encouraged to scream. The Bradley method also devotes a lot of attention to exercise and nutrition. Over 90 percent of Bradley graduates have "natural" births. Bradley was the original "husband-coached" childbirth method and does more to include the father than any of the other methods.

KITZINGER PSYCHO-SEXUAL British-born educator Sheila Kitzinger believes that pleasurable sexual sensations can be aroused during the birth process and that these sensations can be used to relax laboring women. Kitzinger also believes that the home birth is the best way to go since birth is a family process and everyone should be involved.

LEBOYER Hospital delivery rooms are usually bright, noisy places. Dr. Leboyer, a French obstetrician, contends that these circumstances are quite stressful and upsetting for a newborn. Leboyer babies are generally born in dimmed rooms, with the mother fully or partially submerged in warm water.

"Coach"—Don't Use That Word

Almost all of the most common childbirth methods refer to the man as the childbirth "coach"—a term that seems to have been coined by Dr. Robert Bradley, the founder of the Bradley method. Today most expectant fathers (at least those who take childbirth classes) and their partners view themselves in those terms, but I agree with Professor Katharyn May that there are some very compelling reasons to erase the word from your nonsports vocabulary.

- The coach concept focuses attention on the father's role only during the brief period of labor and delivery, and minimizes the important role he plays during the entire pregnancy and beyond.
- The coach concept reinforces the sexist stereotype of the father as a prop, and dehumanizes him as a unique individual in the process of sharing a challenging life experience with his partner. It also places too much pressure on the father by implying that he should be providing direction if things go badly during labor and birth.

So, if anyone calls you "coach," tell them you're not—you're the child's *father.*

DICK-READ This method was developed by an English obstetrician named Grantley Dick-Read. He believed pain in labor was caused by images women learned through their culture. His classes comprise three main components:
- Learning the anatomy and physiology of childbirth to dispel the idea that birth must be painful.
- Physical relaxation, physical conditioning, and breathing exercises.
- A therapeutic relationship between the mother and the doctor that gives the mother faith in the doctor, allaying her fear and making it easier for her to relax.

Childbirth classes usually run five to nine weeks (if you're really short on time, you may be able to find an intensive two- or three-day program) and typically cost $75 to $100 for the whole course. Your practitioner or the maternity ward of the hospital in which you're planning to deliver are good sources for information on where childbirth classes meet and how to sign up.

Baby CPR
Another class you should try to fit in this month is baby CPR (if you wait until after the baby comes, you'll never get around to it). Hopefully, you'll never have to use the skills you'll learn, but it's important to learn them—for your own peace of mind and for your baby's safety. You can find out where to sign up from your birth class instructor, your baby's pediatrician (if you've picked one already), the hospital where the baby will be born, or your local American Red Cross Community Education Center.

GETTING THE MOST OUT OF THE CLASS
While you should definitely take a birthing class, there's one essential thing you should know about them: the focus is exclusively on your partner—what *she's* going through, what *she's* feeling, and what you can do to help her. All these things are very important, but you might still reasonably ask, "What about me?" Reading this book will help you prepare yourself for the emotional and physical experiences you'll be going through during pregnancy and birth. But while you and your partner are actually going through labor, you are *both* in a state of trauma. You're *both* under pressure and you *both* need support—physical as well as psychological.

Each time my wife was in labor, I tried to do everything they'd taught me

What Childbirth Classes Don't Teach You

While childbirth education classes are an important part of the birthing experience, there are a few things you probably won't learn there.

- **Ask a lot of questions.** No matter how much you've read or how thorough your class is, something you don't understand is bound to happen during the labor or delivery. When it does, don't let the hospital staff steamroller you. Have them explain everything they're doing, every step of the way. If you miss something the first time, have them explain it again.

- **Stand up for your rights.** Most couples have a tendency to step back and let the practitioners take control of their labor or delivery, especially when something unusual happens. They feel out of place and unsure of their rights. Don't. This is your partner's and your labor and delivery—not the doctor's or the nurse's—and you have the right to have things done the way you want them done.

- **Don't take no for an answer.** Often, the first thing out of a doctor's or nurse's mouth when you ask for something is "No"—not because it's the right answer, but because it's the easy answer. If you want the lights dimmed for the delivery and the staff refuses, dim them yourself. If you want to videotape the birth and the doctor won't let you, demand an explanation. If you don't get a good one, do what *you* feel you should do.

in the classes we'd taken: I reassured her, held her, told her stories, massaged her back and legs, mopped her brow, and fed her ice chips. But there was no one to reassure me or hold me when I was feeling frightened. And neither this nor any other book can do that for you.

Fortunately, however, there *is* a way to help ease the burden—both yours and hers—of the trauma of labor and delivery: get yourselves a *doula*.

WHAT IS A *DOULA*?

Doula is a Greek word that means "a woman caregiver of another woman." Most doulas have had children of their own, and all of them go through an intensive training period in which they are taught how to give the laboring woman *and* her partner emotional and physical support throughout labor, as well as information about the delivery.

Doulas—Some Basic Q's and A's

♦ **What do doulas charge?** Most doulas charge a flat fee ranging from $200 to $600.

♦ **Will my insurance company pay for a doula?** There's no hard and fast rule about this. But more and more insurance companies are finding that paying for a doula can significantly reduce their other birth-related costs.

♦ **Where can I find one?** Your OB, hospital, or local chapter of the LaLeche League should be able to help you locate one. You also can contact Doulas of North America, 1100 23rd Avenue East, Seattle, WA 98112. Fax (206) 325-0472.

According to Dr. Marshall Klaus, the doula concept is not new. For hundreds of years, pregnant women in more than 125 cultures have gone through labor with another woman at their side the whole time. This used to be the case in the United States as well. But in the 1930s women began to have their children in hospitals instead of at home, and everyone but the laboring woman and her doctors was barred from the delivery room. In 1980, however, Dr. Klaus and his colleagues reintroduced the doula concept in the U.S. and gave it its name.

I've got to confess that when I met with Dr. Marshall Klaus, my first reaction was: no way. I've got too much invested in this pregnancy, and nobody is going to come between me and my wife during this critical stage. But as I continued talking to Dr. Klaus and reading the research on doulas, I began to change my mind.

I learned that the presence of a doula can have some rather dramatic effects on the length of a woman's labor (25 percent shorter), as well as on the odds of her needing pain medication (reduced by up to 47 percent), forceps delivery (reduced by 35 to 82 percent), or a Cesarean section (reduced 34 to 67 percent). Considering my wife's history of long, painful labor, I began to feel that having a doula around the next time might be the way to go.

But what would a doula do for *me*? Wouldn't she just push me out of the way? "The doula is there to help parents have the type of birthing experience they want," says Dr. Klaus. "She will never take over or attempt to control the birth. We make the mistake of thinking that a father can take a birthing class and be prepared to be the main source of support and knowledge for the entire labor. That's just unreasonable. A doula can reach out to the man, decreasing his anxiety, giving him support and encouragement, and allowing him to interact with his partner in a more caring and nurturing fashion."

Many men, even after taking birthing classes, still feel unsure about how they'll "perform" during the labor. Others feel they'd like to be fully involved in the pregnancy, but that labor and delivery are experiences that women are simply better equipped to handle. If you fit into either of these categories, or if you think it might be reassuring to have someone knowledgeable and supportive at your side during labor, consider a doula.

WHAT IF YOU FEEL LIKE YOU DON'T WANT TO BE IN THE DELIVERY ROOM AT ALL?

Years ago, no one expected men to be involved in their partners' pregnancy or to be there for the birth of their children. But today, men who aren't enthusiastically involved are generally regarded as insensitive Neanderthals. "There's a fine line between finding options for father participation, and pressuring men to adopt levels of involvement which may be unwanted or inappropriate for them," says Katharyn May. The truth of the matter is that not all of us feel the same need to be involved, and the *last* place some men should be is in the delivery room.

You may be squeamish during medical procedures or worried about losing control during labor. You may not want to see your partner in pain, or you may simply be feeling ambivalent about the pregnancy. You may even be feeling resentful about the pressure other people are putting on you to get involved. It's important to remember that these—and any other feelings you might have for just not wanting to be there—are not only completely normal, but they're shared by more men than you might think.

If you're feeling less than overjoyed about being involved in the labor and delivery, you might want to consider some of the following suggestions:

- **Talk to other fathers.** Hearing what other men have been through may help you get over some of your concerns. You might also find that you're not alone.
- **Understand what your partner's thinking.** Instead of trying to understand *why* you're feeling the way you do, your partner may interpret your apprehensiveness as a sign that you don't care about her or the baby.
- **Talk to your partner.** Let her know what you're feeling and why. At the same time, reassure her about your commitment to her and to the baby.
- **Do it for her.** No matter how well you explain it to your partner, your desire to miss the birth or to miss the classes is probably going to hurt her. If you can stomach it at all, at least try to take the class—it will

help her feel more understood, and you might just learn what it is that's been bothering you.

♦ **Consider a doula.** See pages 107–9 for information about doulas.

♦ **Don't feel that you're a failure.** You're not. As many as half of all expectant fathers have at least some ambivalence about participating in the pregnancy and childbirth. Being forced into a role that isn't comfortable for you will do you—and your partner—more harm than good.

♦ **Don't give in to the pressure.** If, after everything is said and done, you still don't feel comfortable participating, don't. But be prepared: your family, friends, and medical practitioner will probably suggest that you just quit pouting and do what you're "supposed to."

♦ **Don't worry about how your child will turn out.** While there's plenty of evidence about the positive impact on children of early paternal bonding, your not being there for the actual birth will *not* cripple your children—you'll still be able to establish a strong relationship with them. Just get there as soon as you feel comfortable, and take as active a role as you can handle.

Notes:

Making a List and Checking It Twice

What She's Going Through

Physically

♦ Even stronger fetal activity
♦ Heavier vaginal discharge
♦ General discomfort getting more severe
♦ Frequent urination
♦ Sleeplessness
♦ Increased fatigue
♦ Shortness of breath as the baby takes up more room and presses against her internal organs
♦ Water retention, and swelling of the hands, feet, and ankles
♦ More frequent Braxton-Hicks contractions

Emotionally

♦ Feeling special—people are giving her their seats on buses or in crowded rooms, store clerks go out of their way to help her
♦ Feeling a bond with others, like a member of a secret club (strangers keep coming up to tell her about their own pregnancy experiences or to touch her belly)
♦ Feeling exceptionally attractive—or ugly
♦ Worried about what she's going to do with the baby once it arrives
♦ Worried about whether her body will ever get back to normal
♦ Afraid her water will break in public

What's Going On with the Baby

At this point, most babies will have assumed the head-down position that they'll maintain for the rest of the pregnancy. He or she is getting big and fat—eighteen inches long, five pounds—and his or her movements are so powerful that you can frequently tell which part of the baby's body is doing the poking. The baby can now open his or her eyes and responds differently to your and your partner's voices.

What You're Going Through

Dealing with the "Public" Nature of Pregnancy

As intensely private as pregnancy is, it is also inescapably public. Your partner's growing belly can bring out the best—and the worst—in people. Perfect strangers will open doors for her, offer to help her carry things, give up their seats in crowded subway cars and buses. In some ways, people's interest in pregnant women and in the process of creating life is heartwarming. But there may come a point at which this outpouring of interest in her status and concern for her comfort begins to feel like an invasion of privacy.

People would come up to my wife and start talking to her even when she was standing in the check-out line at the grocery store. The "conversations" would usually start out fairly innocuously, with questions like, "So, when are you due?" or pronouncements about the baby's gender. But after a while the horror stories would inevitably come out—tales of debilitating morning sickness, ten-month pregnancies, thirty-hour labors, emergency C-sections, anesthesia that didn't work, and on and on. And as if that weren't enough, people would, without even asking, start touching, rubbing, or patting her belly.

Perhaps the strangest thing about the public nature of pregnancy is that many women seem to take it all in stride. I kept waiting for my wife to bite some belly-rubber's hand off, but she never did. For some men, however, this touching business can bring out feelings of anger: "Nobody touches my woman!" If this happens to you, it's best to take your cues from your partner. If she doesn't mind, try to relax.

Panic

Just about six weeks before our first daughter was born, I suddenly had a great epiphany: our childless days were about to be over. It wasn't that I was worried about becoming a father—I already felt confident and prepared for my new role: I'd read a lot of material about becoming a parent, my wife and I had been taking childbirth classes, and we'd thoroughly discussed our concerns and fears.

What had struck me was much more superficial: once the baby came, it would be a long time before we'd be able to go to movies, plays, or concerts (or just about anyplace where you might have to be quiet), or even stay out late with our friends.

As it turned out, my wife was feeling the same thing at about the same time, so during the last two months of the first pregnancy, we ate out more often, went to more movies, saw more plays, and spent more late evenings with friends than in the next three years combined.

In addition to trying to pack a lot of fun activities into the last few months of the pregnancy, you might want to consider cramming in a few practical things as well: when you (or your partner) are preparing food, try to double or even triple the recipes and freeze what's left over in two-person servings. Believe me, during that first postpartum week, defrosting some frozen spaghetti sauce is a lot easier than making a new batch from scratch.

Nesting

After morning sickness and 2 A.M. cravings for pickles, perhaps the most famous stereotype about pregnancy is a woman's "nesting instinct." Most women, at some point in their pregnancies, become obsessed (often unconsciously) with preparing the house for the new arrival: closets and cupboards are cleaned, and furniture that hasn't been budged for years suddenly has to be swept under.

Although much has been made of the *woman's* instinct, a variety of studies have shown that almost all expectant fathers experience some sort of nesting

instinct themselves. Besides worrying about finances, many men spend a lot of time assembling—or even building—cribs, changing tables, and other baby furniture; shopping for baby supplies; painting and preparing the baby's room; rearranging furniture in the rest of the house; and even trying to find a larger living space for their growing families.

For some men, these activities are a way to keep busy and to avoid feeling left out. But for others, they represent something much more fundamental. As Pamela Jordan writes, "These nesting tasks may be the first opportunity the father has to do something for the baby rather than his pregnant mate."

Sex—Again

Whereas the second trimester is frequently a time of increased sexual desire and activity, during the third trimester a decrease in sexual relations is not unusual. The most common reasons for this are:

 • A mutual fear of hurting the baby or your partner.
 • Fear that your partner's orgasm might trigger premature labor.
 • Your partner's physical discomfort.
 • Your partner's changing body makes the "usual" sexual positions uncomfortable.
 • Your sense of changing roles. Soon your partner will no longer be only your partner; she's going to be a mother—someone just like your own mother. Remember that as she begins to see you as a father, your partner may have similar (subconscious) thoughts.

Unless your partner's doctor has told you otherwise, sex should pose no physical risk to the baby or to your partner. As discussed on page 81, if you're both still interested in sex, now would be a good time to try out some new and different positions. Again, if you and your partner aren't in sync, sexually speaking, it's critical to talk things through.

Several researchers have noted that a small number of expectant fathers have affairs during the late stages of their partners' pregnancies. But these "late pregnancy affairs" rarely happen for the reasons you might think. Dr. Jerrold Shapiro found that most men who have had a late-pregnancy extramarital affair share the following characteristics:

 • They felt extremely attracted to their partners and were very interested in "affectionate sexual contact" with them.
 • They felt particularly excluded from the pregnancy and birth process.
 • The affair was with a close friend or relative of the woman. (This would indicate that the person with whom the man had the affair

was also feeling excluded from the pregnant woman's life during
the pregnancy.)

Expectant mothers also have affairs during their pregnancies. In fact,
Dr. Shapiro suggests that women are just as likely to have affairs as men.
Couples who suddenly find themselves with no sexual outlet—and are feeling pushed away or misunderstood by their partners—may be tempted to
satisfy their needs elsewhere.

Birth Plans

The notion that an expectant couple has some choice in the labor, delivery,
and the immediate postpartum-period procedures is a fairly recent one. And
while you may be tempted just to "leave things up to the professionals" at the
hospital, you'll have a much better—and less stressful—birthing experience
if you and your partner spend some time thinking about what you really want,
and writing up a *birth plan.*

A birth plan is a good way for you and your partner to make decisions and
set goals for the labor and delivery while you still have clear heads. Remember, though, that things rarely, if ever, go the way they're supposed to. So, be
flexible. Also, be sure to discuss your plan with your practitioner and with the

Sample Birth Plan

This birth plan outlines our desires for this labor, birth, and postpartum
period. These plans can be revised for medical reasons, should some
complication arise, after informed consent has been well established.

 ◆ Mother will be free to move during labor and birth to any position she
   prefers or finds helpful to the birthing process.
 ◆ We would prefer that no pain medication be routinely offered. If the
   mother wants something, she'll ask for it.
 ◆ No episiotomy will be performed; a tear is acceptable if unavoidable.
 ◆ The baby will be given directly to the mother after birth.
 ◆ The baby will be with at least one of his or her parents at all times.
 ◆ Father would like to "catch" the baby as he or she emerges.
 ◆ Father will cut the cord, but not until it stops pulsing.

We would like to thank everyone involved for their support and cooperation during this birth.

hospital. There may be certain policies that can't be breached. Here are some topics you may want to cover in your plan:

- **Pain medication.** Do you want the hospital staff to offer it if they feel your partner could use some? Or do you want them to wait for her to ask for it?
- **Staying together.** Do you and your partner want to remain together for the entire labor and delivery?
- **Freedom of movement.** Will you be able to labor in the hallways (or in the shower), or will your partner have to stay in bed?
- **Labor.** Do you want to be able to select your own positions? If labor slows down, do you want to be offered oxytocin or other drugs to speed it up?
- **Shaving.** Does your partner want her pubic area shaved or left alone? (There's no real reason to shave her if she doesn't want it done.)
- **Pictures and videos.** Do you want to take them? Do you want someone else to? Do you want to be able to take them even if there's a C-section?
- **Fetal monitoring.** Does your partner want to be hooked up to machines throughout her labor, or would she prefer that monitoring be done only when necessary?
- **The birth.** Do you want the doctors to try forceps or suction to speed up the delivery, or do you want to hold out for a while longer? Do you want any other people (friends, relatives, midwife, other children) to attend the birth? Will a mirror be available (so your partner can get a better view of the birth)?

- **Episiotomy.** Do you want the OB to do one as a preventative measure, or is a small tear preferable?
- **Cesarean section.** In case of a C-section, can you stay with your partner, or will you have to be separated? Will you be separated only for the spinal anesthesia, or for the entire procedure? Where will you be allowed to stand?
- **The baby.** Who will cut the cord, and when? Do you want the hospital staff to take the baby away for cleaning and testing right after birth, or would you like him or her handed to you first?
- **After the birth.** Do you want the baby to breastfeed right away, or will you be bottle feeding? Do you want the baby with one of you all the time, or would you rather have him or her kept in the hospital's nursery? What about circumcision?
- **Going home.** Do you want to stay for as long as the hospital will let you, or do you want to go home as soon as possible?

Should Your Older Children Attend the Birth?

Having older children attend the birth of the new baby can be a tricky thing. In general, it's probably okay to have children present both during labor and immediately *after* the birth. But for a variety of reasons, children—especially those under five—probably shouldn't be there for the birth itself.

- They may be frightened that their mother is being hurt, and that all of the blood and moaning might mean she is dying.
- Even well-prepared children can have unpredictable reactions, and you and your partner won't want to have to be distracted by anyone else's needs but yours (and the new baby's).
- The older child might be jealous of all the attention paid to the new baby.

If you're still thinking about having an older child there for the birth of his or her new sibling, be sure to discuss the idea with your doctor first. Then, get yourselves some visual aids—books, movies, or pictures of births, for example—and plan on having some long discussions with the child. *Birth: Through Children's Eyes,* edited by Sandra Van Dam Anderson and Penny Simkin (P. T. Pennypress, 1981), is a good resource.

Birth instructor Kim Kaehler suggests that you keep the following points in mind when writing your plan:

♦ In the opening paragraph, indicate your flexibility should a medical emergency arise. But also stress the importance of informed consent.

♦ Try not to make it sound like a legal document. That will make a doctor or other health-care provider very nervous and defensive.

♦ Try to word your desires in a positive way. Avoid beginning every statement with "No" or "Do not."

♦ Refrain from including things in your plan that are not part of your birthplace's normal procedures. (If your hospital doesn't routinely do fetal monitoring, there's no need to mention it.)

♦ Be sure to thank everyone for their cooperation and support.

♦ After you and your partner have hammered out a draft of your birth plan, show it to your doctor. Let him or her go over it and make suggestions.

Making Final Plans

REGISTERING AT THE HOSPITAL

Despite what you've seen on TV and in the movies, getting to the hospital doesn't have to be a frantic exercise at breakneck speed. Fortunately for men (but not nearly as fortunately for our partners), the onset of labor and the delivery itself are usually hours (if not days) apart, so if you plan carefully, there should be plenty of time to get everything done. And once you've got your bags packed and ready to go (see pages 121–22 for details), the next most pressing concern is registering at the hospital.

Most hospitals will allow—or may even require—you to register up to sixty days before the anticipated birth of the child. This doesn't mean that you're making a reservation for a particular day. All it means is that when you do show up at the hospital, you won't have to waste time signing papers while your partner is having contractions. So check with your hospital's or clinic's administrative offices as soon as you can. Doing so is particularly important because besides making you fill out 785 forms, the hospital will have to get a verification of coverage and eligibility from your insurance company. And that can take some time.

FINDING A PEDIATRICIAN

During their first year, both my daughters saw their pediatrician nine times—and they were both healthy. You can expect visits every two weeks for the first month, monthly or every other month until six months, once in the ninth month, and again in the twelfth month. Clearly, since you're going to be spending a lot of time with your child's doctor, you should select someone you think you can get along with. It's perfectly acceptable to interview several prospective pediatricians, and if you do, here are some questions you should ask:

♦ **What insurance plans do you participate in?**

♦ **What is your philosophy about vaccinations?** Although the vast majority of pediatricians advocate routine vaccination, there is a vocal minority that doesn't. The debate is interesting but beyond the scope of this book.

♦ **How many doctors are in your practice?** You may think that male and female doctors are the same, but your child may not agree. When she was about two, my older daughter absolutely refused to see her regular (male) pediatrician, and insisted on seeing a "girl doctor." Don't worry about offending your pediatrician—about 75 percent of kids prefer to see a doctor of their own gender.

♦ **Where is your lab work done?** It's a lot faster and cheaper when most routine tests are done right in the office.

♦ **What about emergencies?**

♦ **What about nighttime and weekend hours?**

♦ **What about non-life-threatening emergencies?** During business hours, the practice we go to has a special, free phone line staffed by pediatric nurses who have successfully diagnosed at least 80 percent of the problems we've called about. At about $50 per visit to the doctor, I can't tell you how much money this has saved us.

GETTING TO THE HOSPITAL

Sooner or later—unless you're planning to have a home birth—you and your partner are going to have to get to the hospital. There are several ways of getting there, each with its own advantages and disadvantages:

♦ **Walking** If you live close enough to the hospital, walking may be the best option. You won't have to worry about any of the disadvantages of driving yourself or getting a ride (see below). You will, however, have to deal with the possible embarrassment of having people stare at you as your partner leans up against the side of a building every three minutes and groans. But your partner may actually like this option since walking can help make the contractions of early labor easier to cope with.

If you're walking, be sure to bring enough cash to take a cab—just in case things don't go the way they should.

ARE WE
THERE
YET ?
½ MILE

DAVE CARPENTER...

+ **Driving yourself** No matter how much you've prepared, when labor really starts, you're going to be a little nervous, and that could be dangerous when you're behind the wheel of a car. You could get lost, get caught speeding, or even cause an accident. And worst of all, if your eyes and mind are on the road, they can't be where they really ought to be— with your partner. Then, when you finally get to the hospital, you'll have to deal with parking—and later retrieving—the car.

If you're driving, make sure you have a full tank of gas, that you know the route (and several alternatives) well, and that you allow enough time to get there. Also, check with the hospital parking lot (if they have one) to find out their rates and hours of operation.

+ **Getting a ride—taxi, friend, or relative** If you're in the back seat of someone else's car, you'll at least be able to tend to your partner. Problems might arise, however, if your partner goes into labor at 2 A.M. and your friends or in-laws take more than a minute or two to roll out of bed. In addition, since most people have never driven a pregnant woman to the hospital, they'll be at least as nervous (probably more) than you would have been. And watch out for potholes; my wife assures me they're hell for a laboring woman.

If you're taking a taxi, have the phone numbers of at least three companies who can get a cab to your door within minutes, at any hour of the day or night. Also, be sure to have enough money for the fare. If you're planning on having someone else do the driving, make sure you have a few backups.

WHAT IF YOU HAVE OTHER KIDS?

If you have other kids—especially young ones—getting to the hospital can be doubly stressful and requires extra planning.

Toward the end of my wife's second pregnancy, we decided that we'd take a cab to the hospital. We also decided that if my wife went into serious labor in the middle of the night, we'd signal our friends who had agreed to take care of our older daughter by calling them, letting their phone ring once, hanging up, calling again, and letting it ring three times.

So, at one in the morning, we made the phone calls, got into the cab, and arrived at our friends' house, where, holding thirty-five pounds of sleeping deadweight, I pounded on the door for five minutes before giving up (our friends had apparently slept through the secret signals). Fortunately, we'd made a backup plan, and when we got to the hospital, we called my parents and had them take their grandchild to their house.

AND FINALLY, SOME LAST-MINUTE DETAILS

+ Keep your doctor's number by the phone.
+ Keep your gas tank full. Have an extra set of keys stashed someplace, or cash for a cab ready.
+ Make sure you've checked to see whether there are any road closures or construction projects along your route to the hospital.
+ Get ready at work. Labor usually starts without warning and can last a long time—sometimes more than a day. Be sure you've delegated urgent matters to a coworker or supervisor, and that your time-off plans are in order. (See pages 88–93 for more on work/family concerns.)

Packing Your Bags

FOR HER

+ A favorite picture on which to focus during labor.
+ Tape player and some favorite tapes to help you both relax during labor.
+ A bathrobe she won't mind getting covered with blood.
+ A large gym bottle (you know, the kind with the built-in straw) for sipping clear liquids.
+ Warm socks and/or old slippers (again, ones she won't mind getting bloody).

♦ Change of clothes to go home in—*not* what she was wearing before she got pregnant. Sweats or maternity pants are particularly good.

♦ Nursing bra.

♦ Her toiletries bag. Don't forget things like mouthwash, toothbrush and toothpaste, contact lens paraphernalia, hairbrush or comb, and a hair ribbon or two.

♦ Box of heavy-duty maxi-pads (unless your partner doesn't mind the kind with the belt, which is what she'll get at most hospitals).

FOR YOU

♦ Comfortable clothes.

♦ Some magazines or a collection of your partner's favorite short stories to read to her.

♦ A swimsuit (you might want to get into the shower with your partner, and the nursing staff might be surprised at the sight of a naked man).

♦ Camera *and* film.

♦ This book.

♦ A cooler filled with snacks. You're not going to want to leave your partner, midcontraction, to run down to the hospital cafeteria. If you have some extra room, a small birthday cake and maybe even some champagne will add a festive touch.

♦ Cash. Depending on the hospital, you may have to leave a cash deposit for phone or television rental. You'll probably need to pay for parking your car or for the taxi ride. You might also need a supply of quarters if you have to use a pay phone.

♦ Phone numbers of the people you'll want to tell the news to right away.

♦ Phone company credit card.

♦ Tennis balls for back rubs.

♦ Toothbrush, extra underwear, shaving kit, and the like. You'll probably end up staying at least one night.

FOR THE BABY

♦ An infant car seat (if you don't have one, the hospital won't let you leave).

♦ A little outfit to go home in—a sleeper or sleep-sac is fine. (It's a good idea to wash *all* new clothes before putting them on the baby.)

♦ Diapers (and pins or diaper wraps if you're using cloth).

♦ Several receiving blankets, weather-appropriate.

The Nursery: Everything You Need and What It Costs

When acquiring anything for your baby, safety should be your primary concern. So before you spend a fortune on Queen Victoria's original bassinet or drag out the crib that you (or your parents or grandparents) slept in as a kid, consider this: your baby will do just about everything possible to jeopardize

Essentials to Have Waiting at Home

FOR THE BABY
- Enough diapers to last for at least a week (you're not going to want to go shopping)
- Baby soap and shampoo
- Thermometer (digital is easiest)
- An ear bulb (These are usually used for rinsing adults' ears, but for babies, they're used for suctioning mucous from their noses. Well, what do you expect? They can't do it themselves!)
- Nail scissors (essential: a baby's nails are like tiny razors and grow like Jack's beanstalk)
- Cotton swabs and alcohol for umbilical cord dressing
- Three or four undershirts
- Three or four sleepers
- Three or four coveralls with snaps
- Sun or snow hat
- Snowsuit (as needed)
- Bottles and formula—even if breastfeeding, just in case . . .
- Three or four baby blankets

FOR YOUR PARTNER
- Nursing pads
- More maxi-pads (she may need these for weeks)
- Any medication or dressing materials needed in the event of a C-section or episiotomy
- Milk and vitamins, especially if she is nursing
- Flowers, and favorite chocolates or other foods she might have avoided during pregnancy
- A good book about your baby's first year of life

A SOFA FOR EVERY BUDGET!

$67.50 $859.35 $64,242,906.25

his or her own life, from sticking his head between the bars of a crib to burying herself under a pile of blankets left in the corner.

New baby furniture must comply with the most recent safety standards. For some guidance on the safest—and best-quality—deals, consult the *Consumer's Guide to Baby Products*.

There are literally hundreds of things you could buy for your newborn's nursery, but here are some of the items you'll need to get the soonest. The prices are retail; you can probably save up to 80 percent by buying these things at garage sales, from friends, or at used furniture stores. But before you get *anything* secondhand, make sure it meets with the safety considerations outlined below.

BABY FURNISHINGS

CRIB: $100 to $600. There's nothing that says *baby* quite like a crib. And so it's no surprise that this is one of the first pieces of baby furniture an expectant couple thinks about. Here are some safety tips:

♦ Get rid of corner posts. Babies can accidentally strangle themselves if their clothes become caught on a post. New cribs are constructed without them, but if you have your heart set on using a vintage model, you should unscrew or saw off the posts.

♦ Slats or bars should be spaced no more than 2⅜ inches apart, and none should be broken or missing.

♦ Never place your crib near draperies, blinds, or anything else that has long, wall-mounted cords. Babies can tear these down or become entangled in them.

CRIB MATTRESS: $100 to $150. Couples are often surprised that mattresses are usually sold separately from the crib. The theory is that some

babies prefer firm mattresses while others prefer softer ones. Don't skimp on mattresses—there's no reason why the one you buy now shouldn't last you through several kids. Just make sure you get a plastic mattress protector.
A few safety tips:

♦ The firmer the better. Studies have shown that there is an increased risk of SIDS (Sudden Infant Death Syndrome) if the mattress is too soft. For the same reason, pillows should never be placed in cribs.
♦ The mattress must fit tightly into the crib (no more than two fingers' width between the edge of the mattress and the side of the crib).

CRIB ACCESSORIES
♦ Crib sheets: $20 to $60.
♦ Bumper: $100 (optional). Even though they can't move very well, babies somehow manage to ram their heads against the sides of the crib—hard enough to leave an impression of the slats or bars on their foreheads. It supposedly reminds them of the feeling of having their heads smashed up against your partner's pubic bone for the last month or two of pregnancy.
♦ Dust ruffle: $80 (optional).
♦ Comforter: $80.
♦ Mobile: $35 to $90 (optional). Some of the most beautiful (and most expensive) mobiles are made to be looked at from the side—where the person who bought it is standing. So remember whom the mobile is really for, and think about whether your baby is really going to be interested in looking at the bottom of a bunch of cars or the underside of a group of jungle animals. In fact, infants can't make out specific shapes for quite some time; experts believe, however, that they can distinguish bold, contrasting colors, and that is why black-and-white mobiles seem to please them the most.

BASSINET: $80 to $150. For the first few months of your baby's life, you may want him or her to sleep in the bedroom with you. If nothing else, this arrangement will make breastfeeding a lot more convenient.

Bassinets can generally accommodate a baby until he or she is about three months old. They come in a variety of styles (wheels, no wheels, handles, no handles, rocking, nonrocking).

CAR SEAT: $40 to $100. A car seat may be the most indispensable baby item. (Again, you won't be able to take your baby home from the hospital without one.) You may want to consider getting two car seats—a small one (perhaps with handles so you can carry the baby around with you) that can be used until the baby reaches twenty pounds, and a larger one for later.

CHANGING TABLE: $70 to $200. Changing tables come in an unbelievable variety of sizes and configurations. Some have drawers so that they can be used as a dresser when your child no longer needs to be changed. The problem with drawers, however, is that you have to remember to take out what you need *before* you get started; when you're in the middle of changing the baby, the last thing you want to be doing is fumbling around blindly for a clean outfit. Be sure to get a foam pad for the top of the table and a couple of washable pad covers. You also should stock your changing table with a good supply of the following:

♦ Diapers
♦ Baby wipes
♦ Diaper rash ointment, such as A&D or Desitin
♦ Cotton swabs and alcohol for cleaning the umbilical cord stump
♦ Baby shampoo and soap (a mild one like Neutrogena or Dove is best)

Note: Stay away from baby powder. Most pediatricians believe that the dust could be harmful to babies.

PORTABLE PLAYPEN: $80 to $150. This is perfect for children less than thirty-four inches tall and lighter than about thirty pounds. Not only does it fold up compactly enough to check as luggage when you're traveling, but it can also be used at home. Some of our friends' children essentially lived in their playpens for the first eighteen months of their lives.

STROLLER: $100 to $600. A good stroller can make life worth living, and you shouldn't waste your time or your money on one that won't last. We took our older daughter and her stroller all over the world, and the stroller is still in perfect condition. Getting a quality stroller doesn't mean you have to buy the one with every available option. Stick to the basics, such as weight, ease of folding, brakes, and balance (you don't want the thing tipping over backward with your baby in it). Finally, make sure the handles are long enough for *you* to push the stroller when you're standing up straight. Most strollers are made to be used by women, which means that if you're over 5'7" or so, you'll have to stoop a little to push. You might not notice it at first, but after a while, your back may give you trouble. Handle extenders cost about $20 and are a great investment. City dwellers who do a lot of traveling on subways or buses will want a sturdy but collapsible stroller—preferably one that you can fold with one hand while holding the baby with the other. Otherwise, it's next to impossible to get onto public transportation (at least without annoying everyone behind you).

BATHTUB: $20. A small plastic washbasin is best for newborns because a sink is too big and can be dangerous. When the baby outgrows the basin, you can soak his or her little formula-stained clothes in it.

DIAPERS: A few years ago, no one would have thought that diapers would become a political issue or that something so insignificant could make or break friendships, but they have. Here are the basic arguments:

Disposable diapers account for more than 1 percent of the nation's landfill. They're made of plastic and will stay in their present form for thousands of years. "Biodegradable" diapers, which break down after only five hundred years, are available in many cities.

Cloth diapers, in contrast, are all natural. The problem is that they're made of cotton, which is taxing on farmland. And in order to sterilize them properly, diaper services wash them seven times (it's true) in near-boiling water, thereby consuming a tremendous amount of power, water, and chemical detergents. The clean diapers are then driven all over town in trucks that fill the air with toxic pollutants.

The choice is yours.

My wife and I started out by using cloth diapers for our older daughter. But I noticed that every time my daughter filled one up, it had a nasty tendency to siphon the contents immediately away from the baby and onto my pants— not pleasant—and that meant even more laundry! It's possible that this phenomenon was the fault of my poor diapering technique. But I'm convinced that disposables, which have elastic around the leg openings, do a better job of keeping the contents in place.

♦ **Disposable diapers:** $8 to $9 for 50. Since you'll be using 5 to 8 diapers a day, this option can get pretty pricey. But if you keep your eyes out for coupons (most parenting magazines have a bunch of them in every issue), you can save a lot. In addition, places like Toys "Я" Us have generic or house brands that are a lot cheaper and usually just as good.

Some people say that kids who grow up with disposable diapers tend to become potty trained later than those who use cloth. Apparently, the disposable kind keep so much moisture away from the baby's bottom that the baby stays comfortable for a longer time.

♦ **Cloth diapers:** about $12 for a package of six. The availability and cost of diaper cleaning services vary greatly around the country. If you sign up with a diaper service, you'll probably start with about eighty diapers per week. If you're doing your own laundry, you should buy about forty.

Even if you don't end up using cloth diapers for the baby, you should still buy a dozen anyway—they're great for drying baby bottoms on changing tables and for draping over your shoulder to protect your clothes when your baby spits up.

FORMULA: Prices vary. You can use powdered, full-strength liquid, or liquid concentrate. But when you start checking formula prices, your partner may decide to keep breastfeeding a while longer. When we weaned our daughters, we put them on the powdered formula—I made a pitcher of it every morning and kept it in the refrigerator.

Notes:

"Dear, It's Time…"

What She's Going Through

Physically

♦ Some change in fetal activity—the baby is so cramped that instead of kicking and punching, all he or she can do is squirm

♦ Increased sleeplessness and fatigue

♦ A renewed sense of energy when the baby's head "drops" into the pelvis and takes some of the pressure off

♦ Just plain miserable—increased cramping, constipation, backache, water retention, and swelling of the feet, ankles, and face

Emotionally

♦ More dependent on you than ever— afraid you won't love her after the baby is born (after all, she's not the same woman you married)

♦ Impatient: can't wait for pregnancy to be over

♦ Short-tempered: tired of answering "So when's the baby coming?" questions—especially if she's overdue

♦ May be afraid she won't have enough love to go around—what with loving you, and all

♦ Fear she won't be ready for labor when it comes

♦ Increasing preoccupation with the baby

What's Going On with the Baby

Over the course of this last month of pregnancy, your baby will be growing at a tremendous clip. Before he or she finally decides to leave the warm uterus, he or she will weigh six or seven pounds, if not more, and be about twenty inches long—so big that there will be hardly any room for him or her to kick or prod your partner. Fingernails and toenails are frequently so long they have to be trimmed right after birth.

What You're Going Through

Confusion

Well, it's almost over. In just a few weeks, you're finally going to meet the child you've talked to and dreamed about, and whose college education you've planned. But be prepared; the last month of pregnancy is often the most confusing for expectant fathers. At times you may be almost overcome with excitement and anticipation. At other times you may be feeling so scared and trapped that you want to run away. In short, all the feelings—good and bad— that you've experienced over the last eight months are back. But now, because of the impending birth, they're more intense than before. Here are a few of the contradictory emotional states you may find yourself going through during the final stages of the pregnancy:

♦ On the one hand, you may be feeling confident about your readiness to be a father. On the other, you may be worried and unsure about whether you'll be able to handle your dual roles as husband and father.

♦ If you've taken on a second job or increased responsibilities at work, all you'll probably want to do at the end of the day is go home and relax. But with your partner less and less able to handle physical tasks, you may be greeted at the door with a list of chores that need to be done.

♦ You and your partner may be feeling an exceptionally strong emotional bond with each other. At the same time, your sex life may have completely disappeared.

♦ As your partner gets more and more uncomfortable, she may feel less and less like going out with friends, so the two of you may be spending a lot more time together. This may be the last chance you have to enjoy some quiet, private time before the baby comes. But it may also be an unwelcome opportunity to get on each other's nerves.

♦ You may find yourself spending a lot more time with friends and family members who have small children, or you may find yourself avoiding families with kids.

Increased Dependency on Your Partner

By this time your attention—and that of your friends and family—is focused squarely on your partner and the baby. Since you're the person she's closest to and sees most often, your partner is going to be increasingly dependent on you—not only to help her physically, but to get her through the last-month emotional ups and downs. At the same time, though, you are going to be increasingly dependent on her as you get onto the last-month roller coaster.

Your partner's increased dependency is considered a "normal" part of pregnancy. But thanks to the ridiculous, gender-specific way we socialize people in this country, men are supposed to be independent, strong, supportive, and impervious to emotional needs—especially while their partners are pregnant. So, just when you are feeling most vulnerable and least in control, your needs are swept under the rug. And what's worse, the one person you most depend on for sympathy and understanding may be too absorbed in what's going on with herself and the baby to do much for you.

This results in what Dr. Luis Zayas calls an "imbalance in interdependence," which leaves the father to satisfy his own emotional needs *and* those of his partner. In addition, in many cases this imbalance essentially becomes a kind of vicious circle that "accentuates the stress, intensifies feelings of separation, and heightens dependency needs." In other words, the less response you get to your dependency needs, the more dependent you feel.

Feeling Guilty

Especially in the last month or so of the pregnancy, many men begin to feel guilty about what they think they've been putting their partners through. Yes, you're the one who got her pregnant, and yes, she's uncomfortable as hell. But strange as it might seem to you, your partner does not blame you for what she's going through. She understands and accepts—as you should—that this was her idea, too, and that (at least short of surrogate motherhood or adoption) there's simply no way to have a baby without going through this. So quit torturing yourself—there are a lot more productive things you can be doing with your time during these last few weeks.

Staying Involved

Sensitivity

The bottom line is that during the last few weeks of her pregnancy, your partner is likely to be miserable and uncomfortable. And although there's not a whole lot you can do to ease her burden, here are a few suggestions that might make the final stretch a little more bearable—for both of you:

♦ Answer the phone. If you have an answering machine, you might consider changing the recording to something like: "Hi. No, we don't have a baby yet, and yes, Jane's fine. If you're calling about anything else, please leave a message and we'll call you back." That may sound a little snotty, but believe me, it's a lot less snotty than *you* would be if you were really answering the same questions twenty times a day.

♦ Stay nearby whenever you can. Try to come home a little earlier from work, give away those basketball tickets, and postpone that long business trip.

♦ Stay in touch. A couple of quick calls to her every day can make her feel loved and important. They'll also reassure her that *you* are all right. If you need to be away from the phone, consider getting a pager or a cellular phone.

♦ Stay as calm as you can. She'll be nervous enough for both of you.

♦ Be patient. She may do some pretty bizarre things, and the best thing you can do is bear with her. If the house has already passed the white-glove test and the car has been waxed twice, and she wants it all done over again, do it—she needs the rest.

♦ Review the breathing, relaxation, and any other techniques you plan to use during labor.

♦ If she wants it, give her some time to herself. And if she wants time with you, make sure you're there for her.

In addition, now would be an appropriate time to reread the "Ways to Show Her You Care" section on pages 67–68.

What If She's Overdue?

There's nothing more frustrating than starting the tenth month of a nine-month pregnancy. You've already given up answering the phone, afraid it's another one of those "What are *you* doing at home? I was sure you'd be at the hospital by now" calls. And you're sick of ending every conversation at the office with, "Now if I'm not in tomorrow, don't forget. . . ." The empty bassinet looks forlorn, and you're just dying to meet the baby face to little wrinkled face.

In most cases, however, couples who think they're late really aren't. When doctors tell a pregnant woman her due date, they often neglect to add that it's only a ballpark figure based on an assumed twenty-eight-day menstrual cycle. If your partner's cycle is long, short, or irregular, her "official" due date could be off by as much as three weeks. And even if her cycle is like clockwork, it's nearly impossible to tell exactly when you conceived. The

Labor: Real or False

By now, your partner has probably experienced some Braxton-Hicks contractions, often called "false labor." Such contractions essentially warm up the uterus for the real thing. Sometimes, however, these practice contractions may be so strong that your partner may feel that labor has begun.

The bottom line is that when *real* labor starts, your partner will probably know it. (This may sound strange, especially if she is carrying her first child. Nevertheless, the majority of mothers I've spoken to have told me it's true.) But until then, you—and she—may not be sure whether the contractions and other things she's feeling are the real thing or not. So before you go rushing off to the hospital, take a few seconds to try to figure things out.

FALSE LABOR

♦ Contractions are not regular, or don't stay regular

♦ Contractions don't get stronger or more severe

♦ If your partner changes position (from sitting to walking, or from standing to lying down), the contractions usually stop altogether or change in frequency or intensity

♦ Generally, there is little or no vaginal discharge of any kind

♦ There may be additional pain in the abdomen

REAL LABOR

♦ Contractions are regular

♦ Contractions get stronger, longer, and closer together with time

♦ There may be some blood-tinged vaginal discharge

♦ Your partner's membranes may rupture (the famous "water" that "breaks" is really the amniotic fluid that the baby has been floating in throughout the pregnancy)

♦ There will undoubtedly be additional pain in the lower back

bottom line is that "70 percent of post-term [late] pregnancies are due to miscalculations of the time of conception," according to the authors of *What to Expect When You're Expecting*.

While going past the due date by a week or so is usually not a problem, being truly overdue *can* have serious consequences:

♦ The baby can grow so large that he or she will have problems passing through the birth canal, thus increasing the chances of a difficult delivery or a C-section.

♦ After a certain point the placenta gets so old that it can no longer provide adequate nourishment for the baby. This can result in the baby's losing weight in the uterus, increasing the risk of fetal distress.

♦ There may no longer be enough amniotic fluid to support the baby.

♦ There may be inadequate room for the umbilical cord to perform properly.

If your doctor feels the baby is overdue, he or she will most likely prescribe some tests to make sure the baby is still okay. The most common tests are an ultrasound (to determine the level of amniotic fluid as well as to get a general idea of how the baby is doing) and a nonstress test, which monitors changes in the baby's heart rate and movement in reaction to certain stimuli.

If the baby "passes" the tests, the doctor will probably send you home, telling you to repeat the test in a week if the baby hasn't come by then. Otherwise, he or she may suggest that you schedule a date for labor to be induced.

If all of this starts getting you down, remember the words of obstetrician J. Milton Huston of New York Hospital, "In all of my years of practice, I've never seen a baby stay in there."

What If It's a Boy?

If you haven't made up your mind about circumcision yet, now's the time to do so. You may already have strong feelings on the subject. If so, feel free to skip this section. But if you're still undecided, the pros and cons of circumcision are summarized below.

WHY YOU MIGHT WANT TO CONSIDER CIRCUMCISION

♦ **Religious reasons.** Circumcision is a traditional, ritual practice for Jews and Muslims.

♦ **Health.** A 1989 study commissioned by the American Academy of Pediatrics (AAP) found that circumcision may reduce a boy's risk of developing urinary tract infections or cancer of the penis, and may reduce his future partner's chance of developing cancer of the cervix. In addition, circumcision completely prevents *phimosis,* a condition in which the foreskin can't be retracted. Generally, the cure for phimosis (which affects about 10 percent of males) is circumcision, a procedure that gets a lot more painful with age.

- **Hygiene.** A circumcised penis is a lot easier to clean—both for the parents and for the boy himself.
- **Conformity.** If you've been circumcised, your son will probably want to look like you. And because circumcision is so popular in the United States, he'll look more like the other boys in the locker room.

WHY YOU MIGHT WANT TO CONSIDER
NOT CIRCUMCISING YOUR SON

- **Pain.** No matter how you look at it, getting circumcised is painful. The circumcision cut will take about three days to heal fully.
- **Other risks.** Complications, while extremely rare, can occur. The AAP found that there is about a 1 in 500 chance of bleeding or local infection due to circumcision, and that death is almost never a risk. In 1979, for example, there was only one circumcision-related death in the entire United States.
- **Is it necessary?** Some claim that many of the health risks thought to be reduced by circumcision may in fact be reduced simply by better hygiene—something that *can* be taught.
- **Conformity.** As above, if you haven't been circumcised, your son will probably want to look like you.

CARE OF THE CIRCUMCISED PENIS

Your son's penis will be red and sore for a few days after the circumcision. And until it's fully healed, you'll need to protect the newly exposed tip and keep it from sticking to the inside of his diaper (a few tiny spots of blood on his diapers for a few days, however, is perfectly normal). Ordinarily, you'll need to keep the penis dry, and the tip lubricated with petroleum jelly and wrapped in gauze. The person who performed the circumcision or the hospital nursing staff will be able to tell you how long you'll need to keep the penis covered and how often to change the bandages.

CARE OF THE UNCIRCUMCISED PENIS

Even if you elect not to circumcise your son, you'll still have to spend some time taking care of his penis. The standard way to clean an uncircumcised penis is to retract the foreskin and gently wash the head of the penis with mild soap and water. However, 85 percent of boys under six months have foreskins that don't retract, according to the AAP. If this is the case with your son, *do not force it.* Check with your pediatrician immediately and follow his or her hygiene instructions carefully. Fortunately, as boys get older, their foreskins retract on their own; by age one, 50 percent retract, and by age three, 80 to 90 percent.

Dealing with Contingencies

PRETERM LABOR/PREMATURE BIRTH

In the vast majority of pregnancies, labor doesn't start until after the fortieth week. However, a small but significant number of babies (7 to 10 percent) are born prematurely—meaning sometime before the thirty-seventh week. The symptoms of premature labor are exactly the same as those of real labor—they just happen before they're supposed to.

If your partner has any of the following symptoms, she may be considered high risk for premature labor. If you haven't already done so, be sure to let your doctor know whether

- She has an "incompetent cervix"—meaning that the cervix is too weak and may open, allowing the baby to be born too soon. Diagnosed early enough, an incompetent cervix can be "corrected" (and premature births prevented) by sewing the opening of the cervix shut.
- She's had any kind of surgery during pregnancy.
- She's carrying twins (or more).
- She is (or has been recently) a smoker.
- She was exposed to Diethylstilbestrol (DES) while her mother was pregnant with her (many of the daughters of women who took DES to prevent miscarriage were born with abnormalities of the reproductive tract).
- She's had a previous premature labor.
- She's carrying an unusually small fetus.

In most cases, babies born prematurely grow up healthy, but every additional day spent in the uterus significantly increases the chances of survival. Therefore, if your partner shows signs of being in real labor (see page 134 and pages 141–48), call your doctor immediately. If caught early, premature labor can be arrested (usually with the help of intravenous drugs), and the fetus will be able to stay where it belongs for a few more weeks.

After an arrested premature labor, your doctor will most likely order your partner to stay in bed for the rest of the pregnancy. She may even be put on a home fetal monitor to keep an eye on the baby. If this happens, be prepared to step in and take over all of the household responsibilities, as well as responsibility for other children if you have them. If you aren't in a position to do this, you may have to hire someone or ask friends or relatives to help out.

PLANES, TRAINS, AND AUTOMOBILES

It seems like half the births you see in the movies take place on the back seat of a taxi, in a snow-bound cave, or in an airplane bathroom. While those sorts of images may sell movie tickets, the reality is that about 99 percent of babies are born in hospitals, according to the American College of Obstetricians and Gynecologists (ACOG). (And many of the nonhospital births were *planned* that way.) Nevertheless, at some point, just about every pregnant couple starts worrying about giving birth unexpectedly.

EMERGENCY BIRTHS

Emergency births fall into two general categories: either you have a lot of time to prepare (you're snowed in, trapped in your basement because of an earthquake, or shipwrecked—you know you're not going to get to a hospital for a while), or you have little or no time to prepare (you're caught in traffic or your partner's labor was extremely short). Either way, there's very little you can do to get ready.

If you have time, make sure that your partner is in the most sheltered area of wherever you happen to be, and that she's as comfortable as possible. If you have facilities available, boil a piece of string or a shoelace and a pair of scissors or a knife. Then, all you can do is sit tight and let nature take its course.

If you don't have time, try to stay cool. Handling a birth is not as difficult

An Emergency Kit

It's extremely unlikely that your partner will give birth anywhere but in the hospital. However, if you want to make sure all the bases are covered, here's a list of supplies to keep at home, in the car, or anyplace else you and your partner are likely to be spending a lot of time during the last month or so of the pregnancy:

+ Chux pads (large, sterile pads) for absorbing blood, amniotic fluid, and so forth. They're available at medical supply stores. If you can't find Chux pads, newspapers are fine—don't worry, a little ink won't hurt anything.
+ Clean string or shoelaces for tying the umbilical cord, if necessary (see page 140).
+ Clean scissors or knife for cutting the cord, if necessary (see page 140).
+ Some towels to warm the baby and mother after the birth.

as you might think. Doctors who do it for a living, in fact, usually show up just a few minutes before the birth and are there primarily in case any complications arise. Fortunately, full-term babies who seem to be in a hurry to come out usually do so without any complications.

Whether you have time to prepare or not, once the baby starts to come, the procedure for performing a delivery is the same. And you'll know the process has started when

♦ Your partner can't resist pushing.

♦ The baby's head—or any other body part—is visible.

For the rest of this chapter, we'll describe what you should do if there's no way to avoid delivering the baby yourself. The information isn't intended to replace the years of training your doctor or midwife has. So don't try this at home—unless you absolutely have to.

STEP ONE: PREPARATION. Call for help if a phone is available. Try to keep your partner focused on the breathing and relaxation techniques. Put a pillow or some clothing under her buttocks in order to keep the baby's head and shoulders from hitting a hard surface.

STEP TWO: THE HEAD. When the head begins to appear, *do not pull it.* Instead, support it and let it come out by itself. If the umbilical cord is wrapped around the baby's neck, *slowly* and *gently* glide it over the head. Once the head is out, try to remove any mucus from the baby's nose and mouth (although the baby's passage through the birth canal is usually enough to do the trick).

STEP THREE: THE REST OF THE BODY. Holding the baby's head, encourage your partner to push as the baby's shoulders appear. After the head has emerged, the rest of the baby's body should slide out pretty easily.

Immediately place the baby on your partner's chest and encourage her to begin breastfeeding right away. (Breastfeeding makes the uterus contract, which helps expel the placenta and reduces the chances of excessive bleeding.) And don't worry— the umbilical cord is generally long enough to allow the baby to nurse while still attached.

STEP FOUR: THE PLACENTA. Don't think your delivery job is over as soon as the baby's out—the placenta is still to come. *Do not pull on the cord* to "help" things along. After a while the placenta, which is surprisingly large

Cutting the Cord

If you know you can get to a hospital within about two hours, *do not cut the cord.* If you're more than two hours away, however, follow these instructions:

- Using a sterilized piece of string (or, if you have no string, a clean shoelace), tie a tight knot in the cord at least six inches away from the future sight of the baby's navel.
- Tie a second tight knot about two inches farther away.
- Cut the cord *between* the knots with a sterilized pair of scissors or sharp knife.

Things to Remember During an Emergency Birth

- Try to relax. Do everything carefully, thoughtfully, and slowly.
- Call for help as soon as possible.
- Keep the area where the baby will be delivered as clean as possible.
- Baby CPR. If you haven't taken a baby CPR class already, you should really consider it—just in case.

and meaty (it kind of reminds me of a hefty chunk of liver), will emerge on its own. When it does, wrap it up in something clean—but *do not throw it away;* your doctor will want to take a look at it as soon as possible.

After the placenta is out, gently massage your partner's lower abdomen every few minutes. This begins the important process of returning her uterus back to its original shape.

Notes:

Labor and Delivery

What She's Going Through

Labor is generally divided into three stages. The first stage consists of three phases.

STAGE 1

PHASE 1 (EARLY LABOR) can last anywhere from a few hours to several weeks. Your partner can't always feel the contractions. But if she can, they're generally irregular (often 30–40 minutes apart, measured from the time one starts to the time the next one starts) and will last 45–60 seconds. My wife, however, had from 6 to 12 hours of fairly long, fairly regular (3–5 minutes apart) contractions almost every day for a week before our second daughter was born. Your partner may have "bloody show" (a blood-tinged vaginal discharge), backaches, and diarrhea.

PHASE 2 (ACTIVE LABOR) is generally shorter, but far more intense, than the first phase. In the early part of this phase, contractions are about 5 minutes apart and last about 45–60 seconds. If she's been in labor for a while, your partner may be hungry and is still probably able to talk through the contractions. Later in this stage, however, the contractions will get closer together (2–3 minutes apart) and longer (more than 60 seconds). By this time she will have lost her appetite and won't be able to talk through the contractions (she probably won't want to anyway). If you aren't already there, it's time to head off to the hospital.

PHASE 3 (TRANSITION) usually lasts a few hours. You can stop wondering why they call it "labor." Your partner's contractions may be almost relentless—often two or three in a row without a break. She's tired, sweating, her muscles may be so exhausted they're trembling, and she may be vomiting.

STAGE 2 (PUSHING AND BIRTH)
The second stage generally lasts 2–4 hours. This is the shortest and usually the most intense part of the process. Your partner's contractions are still long (more than 60 seconds) but are further apart. The difference is that during the contractions, she'll be overcome with a desire to push—similar to the feeling of having to make a bowel movement.

STAGE 3 (AFTER THE BIRTH)
The baby is born and the placenta needs to be delivered.

What You're Going Through

Starting labor is no picnic, for her or for you. She, of course, is experiencing—or soon will be—a lot of physical pain. You, in the meantime, are very likely to feel a heavy dose of *psychological* pain.

I couldn't possibly count the number of times—only in my dreams, thankfully—I've heroically defended my home and family from armies of murderers and thieves. But even when I'm awake, I know I wouldn't hesitate before diving in front of a speeding car if it meant being able to save my wife or my children. And I know I would submit to the most painful ordeal to keep any one of them from suffering. Somehow just knowing those things, and feeling so sure of what I'd do in a moment of crisis, gives me a strong sense of confidence and control. But helping your partner through labor is not the same as deciding to rescue a child from a burning building.

The most important thing to remember about this final stage of pregnancy is that the pain—yours and hers—is finite. After a while it ends, and you get to hold your new baby. Ironically, however, her pain will probably end sooner than yours. She'll be sore for a few weeks or so, but by the time the baby is six months old, your partner will hardly remember the pain. If women *could* remember the pain, I can't imagine that any of them would have more than one child. But for six months, a year, even two years after our first daughter was born, my wife's pain remained fresh in my mind. And when we began planning our second pregnancy, the thought of her having to go through a remotely similar experience frightened me.

Staying Involved

Being There—Mentally and Physically

Despite your fears and worries, this is one time when your partner's needs—and they aren't all physical—come first. But before we get into how you can best help her through labor and delivery, it's helpful to get a firm idea of how to tell *when* she's actually gone into labor, and what stage she's in once she's there.

STAGE 1: PHASE 1 (EARLY LABOR)

Although the contractions are fairly mild at this point, you should do everything you can to make your partner as comfortable as possible (back rubs, massages, and so forth). Some women may tell you exactly what they want you to do, others may feel a little shy about making any demands—especially things that might seem trivial. Either way, ask her regularly what you can do to help. And when she tells you, do it. If taking a walk makes her feel better, go with her. If doing headstands in the living room is what she wants to do (fairly unlikely at this point), give her a hand. You also need to trust her instincts about what's going on with her body. At some point during every day of my wife's week-long first-stage labor marathon, I became convinced that *this* time it was real and that *this* time she should let me call the doctor. Wisely and firmly, she refused.

Make sure you *both* get something to eat *before* you go to the hospital. In fact, you should bring some food with you. Once you get to the hospital, the nurses won't let your partner eat until after the baby is born, and you're not going to want to try to make a dash to the snack bar between contractions. Finally, try to get some rest. Don't be fooled by the adrenaline rush that will hit you when your partner finally goes into labor. You'll be so excited that you'll feel you can last forever, but you can't. She's got some hormones (and pain) to keep her going; you don't.

STAGE 1: PHASE 2 (ACTIVE LABOR)

One of the symptoms of second-phase labor is that your partner may seem to be losing interest in just about everything—including arguing with you about when to call the doctor. After my wife's contractions had been 2–3 minutes

The Three Stages of Labor and Delivery

STAGE	WHAT'S HAPPENING
Stage 1/Phase 1 (early labor)	<ul><li>Her cervix is effacing (thinning out) and dilating (opening up) up to about 3 centimeters</li><li>Her water may break</li></ul>
Stage 1/Phase 2 (active labor)	<ul><li>She's increasingly uncomfortable</li><li>Her cervix continues to efface and will dilate to about 7 centimeters</li><li>Water may break (if it hasn't already) or may have to be broken</li></ul>
Stage 1/Phase 3 (transition)	<ul><li>Her cervix is now fully dilated</li><li>She may feel the urge to push</li></ul>
Stage 2 (pushing and birth)	<ul><li>Increase in bloody discharge</li><li>The baby is moving through the birth canal</li><li>Doctor may have to do an episiotomy</li></ul>
Stage 3 (after the birth)	<ul><li>The placenta is separating from the wall of the uterus</li><li>Episiotomy or tearing (if any) will be repaired</li></ul>

WHAT SHE'S FEELING	WHAT YOU CAN DO
♦ She may be excited but not totally sure that "this is really it" ♦ She may be anxious and restless ♦ She may not feel like doing much of anything	♦ Reassure her ♦ Tell jokes, take a walk, or rent a movie—anything to distract her
♦ She's getting serious and impatient about the pain ♦ She's beginning to concentrate fully on the contractions	♦ Call the doctor and get her to the hospital ♦ Reassure and encourage her ♦ Help her take one contraction at a time ♦ Feed her ice chips ♦ Praise her for her progress ♦ Massage, massage, massage
♦ She may be confused, frustrated, and scared ♦ She may announce that she can't take it anymore and is going home	♦ Do whatever she wants you to do ♦ Try to help her resist pushing until the doctor tells her she should ♦ Mop her brow with a wet cloth ♦ Feed her ice chips ♦ Massage her (if she wants it)
♦ She's feeling confident that she can finish the job ♦ She may have gotten a second wind	♦ Continue to reassure and comfort her ♦ Encourage her to push when she's supposed to and tell her how great she's doing ♦ Encourage her to watch the baby come out (if she wants to and if there's a mirror around) ♦ Let the professionals do their job
♦ RELIEF ♦ Euphoria ♦ Talkative ♦ Strong, heroic ♦ Hungry, thirsty ♦ Empty (of the baby) ♦ Desire to cuddle with her baby (and her partner)	♦ Praise her ♦ Put the baby on her stomach ♦ Encourage her to relax ♦ Encourage her to start nursing the baby, if she feels ready ♦ Bond with her and the baby

apart for a few hours (and so strong that she couldn't talk through them), I was encouraging her to call. She refused. Many women, it seems, "just know" when it's time to go. So, chances are if she tells you "it's time," grab your car keys. If you're still not sure whether the second phase has started, here's a pretty typical scenario that may help you decide:

YOU: Honey, these contractions have been going on like this for three hours. I think we should head off to the hospital.
SHE: Okay.
YOU: Great. Let's get dressed, okay?
SHE: I don't want to get dressed.
YOU: But you're only wearing a nightgown. How about at least putting on some shoes and socks?
SHE: I don't want any shoes and socks.
YOU: But it's cold out there. How about a jacket?
SHE: I don't want a jacket.

Get the point?

Another typical symptom of second-phase labor is (in most people anyway) an uncharacteristic loss of modesty. Birth-class instructor Kim Kaehler says she can always tell what stage of labor a woman is in just by looking at the sheet on her bed (when she's in it and naked). If she's in first phase, she'll be covered up to her neck; in second phase, the sheet is halfway down; by the third phase (see below), the sheet's all the way off.

STAGE 1: PHASE 3 (TRANSITION)

It seems that when laboring women are shown in TV shows, they're often snapping at their husband or boyfriend, yelling things like "Don't touch me!" or "Leave me alone, you're the one who did this to me." I think I'd internalized those stereotypes and by the time we got to the hospital I was really afraid that my wife would behave the same way when she got to the transition stage, blame me for the pain, and push me away. Fortunately, it never happened. The closest we ever came was when we were in labor with our second daughter. The only place my wife could be comfortable was in the shower, and for a while I was in there with her, trying to talk her through the contractions as I massaged her aching back. Then she asked me to leave the bathroom for a while. Sure, I felt hurt for a minute—I felt I should be there with her—but it was clear that she had no intention of hurting me.

Unfortunately, not every laboring woman manages to be as graceful under pressure. If your partner happens to say something nasty to you or throws you unceremoniously out of the room for a while, you need to imagine that while she's in labor her mind is being taken over by an angry rush-hour mob, all trying to push and shove their way onto an overcrowded subway train. Quite often, the pain she's experiencing is so intense and overwhelming that the only way she can make it through the contractions is to concentrate completely on them. Something as simple and well-meaning as a word or a loving caress can be terribly distracting.

So what *can* you do? Whatever she wants. Fast. If she doesn't want you to touch her, don't insist. Offer to feed her some ice chips instead. If she wants you to get out of the room, go. But tell her that you'll be right outside in case she needs you. If the room is pitch black and she tells you it's too bright, agree with her and find something to turn off. If she wants to listen to the twenty-four-hour Elvis station, turn it on. But whatever you do, don't argue with her, don't reason with her, and above all, don't pout if she swears at you or calls you names. She really doesn't mean to, and the last thing she needs to deal with at this moment of crisis is your wounded pride.

STAGE 2: PUSHING

Up until the pushing stage, I thought I was completely prepared for dealing with my wife's labor and delivery. I was calm, and, despite my feelings of inadequacy, I knew what to expect almost every step of the way. The hospital staff was supportive of my wanting to be with my wife through every contraction. But when the time came to start pushing, they changed. All of a sudden, *they* were in control. The doctor was called, extra nurses magically appeared, and the room began to fill up with equipment—a scale, a bassinet, a tray of sterilized medical instruments, a washbasin, diapers, towels. (We happened to be in a combination labor/birthing room; if, in the middle of pushing, you find yourself chasing after your wife, who's being rushed down the hall to a separate delivery room, don't be alarmed. It may feel like an emergency, but it isn't really.)

The nurses told my wife what to do, how to do it, and when to do it. All I could do was watch—and I must admit that at first I felt a little cheated. After all, *I* was the one who had been with my wife through almost every contraction. *My* baby was about to be born. But when the most important part finally arrived, I wasn't going to be anything more than a spectator. And unless you're a professional birthing coach or a trained labor and delivery nurse, chances are you're going to feel like a spectator, too.

The truth of the matter is that although I was feeling left out and would have liked to have been more involved in this stage, it was probably a lot better for my wife that I wasn't. As I watched the nurses do their stuff, I quickly realized that simply holding your partner's legs and saying, "Push, honey. That's great," just isn't enough. *Recognizing* a good, productive push, and, more important, being able to *explain* how to do one—"raise your butt . . . lower your legs . . . keep your head back . . ."—are skills that come from years of experience.

STAGE 2: BIRTH

Intellectually, I had known my wife was pregnant. I'd been to all the appointments and I'd heard the heartbeat, seen the ultrasound, and felt the baby kicking. Still, there was something intangible about the whole process. And it wasn't until our baby started "crowning" (peeking her hairy little head out of my wife's vagina) that all the pieces finally came together.

At just about the same moment, I also realized that there was one major advantage to my having been displaced during the pushing stage: I had both hands free to "catch" the baby as she came out—and believe me, holding my daughter's hot, slimy, bloody little body and placing her gently at my wife's breast was easily the highlight of the whole occasion.

If you think you might want to do this, make sure you've worked out the choreography with your doctor and the nurses before the baby starts crowning. See "Birth Plans" on pages 115–18 for more information.

Your partner, unfortunately, is in the worst possible position to see the baby being born. Most hospitals, however, have tried to remedy this situation by making mirrors available. Still, many women are concentrating so hard on the pushing that they may not be interested in looking in the mirror.

If you were expecting your newborn to look like the Gerber baby, you may be in for a bit of a shock. Babies are generally born covered with a whitish coating called *vernix*. They're sometimes blue and frequently covered with blood and mucus. Their eyes may be puffy, their genitals swollen, and their backs and shoulders may be covered with fine hair. In addition, the trip through the birth canal has probably left your baby with a cone-shaped head. All in all, it's the most beautiful sight in the world.

After the Birth

THE BABY

Your baby's first few minutes outside the womb are a time of intense physical and emotional release for you and your partner. At long last you get to meet the unique little person you created together. Your partner may want to try nursing the baby (although most newborns aren't hungry for the first twelve

<table>
<tr><td>

Seeing the Baby

Many hospitals have very rigid rules regarding parent/infant contact—feeding may be highly regulated and the hours you can visit your child may be limited. The nursing staff may also bottle-feed the baby—either with sugar-water or with formula. If this isn't what you want, let them know.

Some hospitals, however, are more flexible. The hospital where both our children were born now no longer has a nursery (except for babies with serious health problems). Healthy babies are expected to stay in the mother's room for their entire hospital stay. There are even hospitals that permit the new father to spend the night with his partner and baby. Check with the staff of your hospital to find out their policy.

</td></tr>
</table>

hours or so), and you will probably want to stroke his or her brand-new skin and marvel at his or her tiny fingernails. But depending on the hospital, the conditions of the birth, and whether or not you've been perfectly clear about your desires, your baby's first few minutes could be spent being poked and prodded by doctors and nurses instead of being held and cuddled by you.

At some point after the birth, your baby will be weighed, measured, given an ID bracelet, bathed, diapered, footprinted, and wrapped in a blanket. Some hospitals also photograph each newborn. After that, most hospitals (frequently required by law) apply a silver nitrate gel or drops to your baby's eyes as a protection against gonorrhea. The thing to remember about all this is that in most cases it can—and should—wait.

If, however, your baby was delivered by C-section, or if there were any other complications, the baby will be rushed off to have his or her little lungs suctioned before returning for the rest of the cleanup routine (see page 159 for more on this).

THE PLACENTA

Before our first child was born it had simply never occurred to me (or to my wife, for that matter) that labor and delivery wouldn't end when the baby was born. While you and your partner are admiring your new family member, the placenta—which has been your baby's life support system for the past five months or so—still must be delivered. Your partner may continue to have mild contractions for anywhere from five minutes to about an hour until this happens. The strange thing about this stage of the delivery is that neither you nor your partner will probably even know it's happening—you'll be much too involved with your new baby.

Once the placenta is out, however, you need to decide what to do with it. In this country most people never even see it, and those who do just leave it at the hospital (where it will either be destroyed or, more likely, sold to a cosmetics company—honest). But in many other cultures, the placenta is considered to have a permanent, almost magical bond with the child it nourished in the womb, and disposal is handled with a great deal more reverence. In fact, most cultures that have placenta rituals believe that if it is not properly buried, the child—or the parents, or even the entire village—will suffer some terrible consequences.

Researcher J. R. Davidson found that in rural Peru, for example, immediately after the birth of a child, the father is required to go to a far-off location and bury the placenta deep enough so that no animals or people will accidentally discover it. Otherwise, the placenta may become "jealous" of the attention paid to the baby and may take revenge by causing an epidemic.

In some South American Indian cultures, people believe that a child's life can be influenced by objects that are buried with its placenta. According to Davidson, parents in the Qolla tribe "bury miniature implements copied after the ones used in adult life with the placenta, in the hopes of assuring that the infant will be a good worker. Boys' placentas are frequently buried with a shovel or a pick, and girls' are buried with a loom or a hoe."

But placentas are not always buried. In ancient Egypt, pharaohs' placentas were wrapped in special containers to keep them from harm. And a wealthy Inca in Ecuador built a solid-gold statue of his mother—complete with his placenta in "her" womb.

Even today, the people of many cultures believe that placentas have special powers. In other parts of Peru placentas are burned, the ashes are mixed with water, and the mixture is then drunk by the babies as a remedy for a variety of childhood illnesses. Traditional Vietnamese medicine uses placentas to combat sterility and senility, and in India, touching a placenta is supposed to help a childless woman conceive a healthy baby of her own.

Whatever you and your partner decide to do, it's probably best to keep it a secret—at least from the hospital staff. Some states try to regulate what you can do with a placenta and may even prohibit you from taking it home (although if you really want to, you can probably find a sympathetic nurse who will pack it up for you). We deliberately left our first daughter's placenta at the hospital. But the second one's is still stored in the freezer (we're planning to honor her birth by planting a tree and using the placenta as fertilizer).

Dealing with contingencies

Unfortunately, not all labors and deliveries proceed exactly as planned. In fact, most of them don't. The American Association of Obstetricians and Gynecologists estimates that more than 30 percent of babies are born by Cesarean section. And a good number of mothers who deliver vaginally are medicated in some way. As with so many other aspects of your pregnancy experience, having good, clear information about what's really going on and what the options are during labor and delivery will help you make informed, intelligent decisions about how to handle the unexpected or the unplanned. The key to getting the information you need is to ask questions—and to keep on asking until you're completely satisfied with the answers you're getting. Find out about the risks, the benefits, the effects on your partner, the effects on the baby. The only exception to this rule is when there is a clear medical emergency. In such a case, you might want to save your questions for later.

Here are a few of the contingencies that can come up during the birth and how they might affect you—and your partner.

PAIN MEDICATION

If you've taken a childbirth class (and even if you haven't), you and your partner may have planned to have a "natural" (medication-free) childbirth. Unfortunately, natural childbirth often sounds better—and less painful— than it actually turns out to be. Because your partner is the one who is experiencing the physical pain, you should defer to her judgment when considering pain medication. This doesn't mean, however, that you don't have anything to say about the issue. What you may want to do is discuss her attitude toward medication thoroughly before she's in labor, so you know whether she wants you to suggest it when *you* get concerned, or wait until *she* requests it. And remember, if you do end up having a discussion about medication sometime during labor, make sure you do it in the most supportive possible way. It's painful to have to watch the one you love suffer, but starting an argument when she's in labor isn't a smart idea (and you're not going to resolve anything anyway).

Many women feel that taking pain medication is a sign of weakness, or that they've failed—as women and as mothers. In addition, some childbirth preparation methods view medication as the first step along a path that ultimately leads to Cesarean section. This is not, by any stretch of the imagination, the rule.

Your nurses or doctor may offer you pain relief, or you can request it yourself. We're not suggesting that you should use—or that you will need—pain

Some of the Most Common Options for Relieving Pain

EPIDURAL

An epidural is usually administered during the second stage of labor, when the pain is greatest. Your partner will be asked to lean over a table or lie on her left side. After a local anesthetic has numbed the area, a large needle, through which a catheter carrying the medication is threaded, will be inserted into the space between the spinal cord and the membrane that surrounds it.

ADVANTAGES

♦ The effect is felt almost immediately.

♦ It is the safest, most effective, labor painkiller available.

♦ Very little of the medication "crosses the placenta" (affects the baby).

♦ The medication does not make the mother feel drowsy.

♦ If properly administered (and it usually is), the epidural will block the *pain* of your partner's contractions, while still leaving her able to feel *when* they are starting and, therefore, when to push.

RISKS

♦ Possible increase in maternal blood pressure.

♦ Inability to feel the urge to empty the bladder, which can lead to the need for a urinary catheterization.

♦ If improperly administered, your partner may not be able to feel when to push. This could lead to a forceps delivery (see below), or increase the chance she'll have to have a Cesarean section.

♦ Occasionally causes nausea, headaches, ringing in the ears, or leg cramps.

medication. But whatever you do, knowing a little about your options is always a good idea.

EXHAUSTION

Pain isn't the only reason your partner might need some chemical intervention. In some cases, labor may be progressing so slowly (or be stalled for so long) that your practitioner may become concerned that your partner will be too ex-

DEMEROL

Demerol is usually given through an IV or a shot in the buttocks. It is generally administered no later than three hours before delivery and in conjunction with a tranquilizer (see below).

ADVANTAGES
♦ Takes effect almost immediately.
♦ Generally has little or no effect on your partner's ability to push.

RISKS
♦ Can cause nausea and vomiting.
♦ In larger doses, it can make your partner too drowsy to push effectively.
♦ The medication easily crosses the placenta, causing the baby to be temporarily drowsy at birth, unable to suck properly for a short while, or, in rare cases, unable to breathe without assistance.

SEDATIVES AND TRANQUILIZERS

These do just what you think they might: they relax and calm your partner. They don't have much effect on pain, however.

ADVANTAGES
♦ May relieve anxiety.
♦ If taken in a moderate dose, your partner isn't numbed and can still participate fully in the birth.

RISKS
♦ Can cause nausea and drowsiness.
♦ Cross the placenta and may cause temporary breathing problems and drowsiness in the baby.

hausted by the time she needs to push. This was exactly what happened during our second labor. After twenty hours of labor and only four centimeters of dilation, our doctor suggested pitocin (a drug that stimulates contractions) together with an epidural. This chemical cocktail removed the pain of labor while allowing my wife's cervix to dilate fully and quickly. I'm convinced that this approach not only did not increase the risk of a C-section but actually prevented one by allowing my wife a well-deserved breather before she started pushing.

Other Common Birth Contingencies

FORCEPS

Forceps are long tongs that are used to guide a stubborn baby's head through the birth canal. If the birth is progressing normally, there's no reason to use forceps. Nevertheless, some doctors routinely use them, usually just to increase the speed of delivery. Most forceps deliveries will leave the baby with bruises in the temple area for a week or two. In rare instances, permanent scarring or other damage can occur. In addition, your partner may need additional medication and a larger-than-normal episiotomy (see below). Make sure you ask your doctor—*before* the birth—whether (and if so, how often) he or she uses forceps. Forceps may legitimately be called for if:

♦ The baby is in distress and a vaginal birth needs to be speeded up.

♦ Your partner is too exhausted (or medicated) to push effectively. In this case, using forceps may save your partner from having a C-section.

EPISIOTOMY

An episiotomy involves making a small cut in the perineum (the area immediately below the vagina) to enlarge the vaginal opening and allow for easier passage of the baby's head. About 90 percent of women delivering for the first time under an obstetrician's care have an episiotomy (whether they need it or not). Many women, however, feel that a small amount of tearing is preferable (and less painful) than a routine episiotomy. But the procedure may be legitimately indicated if:

♦ The baby is extremely large, and squeezing through the vagina might harm the baby or your partner.

♦ Forceps are used.

♦ The baby is breech (see below).

BREECH PRESENTATION

If is a baby is breech it means that the feet will be delivered first (only 3–4 percent of babies are born this way). There's nothing you can do to prevent your baby from coming out any way he or she wants to. And in most cases, the fact that the baby is breech doesn't call for any extraordinary measures. Breech presentation does, however, increase your partner's chance of having a C-section.

EXTERNAL AND INTERNAL FETAL MONITORING

This involves attaching a rather complicated machine—complete with graphs, digital outputs, and high-tech beeping—to your partner's abdomen. Fetal monitors are used to monitor your baby's heartbeat and your partner's contractions.

In some respects, fetal monitors are pretty remarkable. If properly hooked up, they are so accurate that by watching the digital display, you will be able to tell when your partner's contractions are starting—even before *she* feels them—and how intense they will be. The forewarning you have may help you coach your partner through the contraction. But if you were thinking that saying something like "Ready, honey? Here it comes—looks like a big one" might be fun, your partner probably won't appreciate the humor.

In many hospitals, laboring women are routinely hooked up to external fetal monitors. Internal fetal monitors (which are actually electrodes attached to the baby's scalp) are also frequently used. But unless there's some compelling reason why you need one (if your partner has been given an epidural, for example, or if there have been signs of fetal distress), you and your partner will be a lot better off without either kind of monitor. Here's why:

- Once the fetal monitor is on, your partner is virtually confined to her bed. No more showers, no more walks to the nursery, no more creative labor positions.
- It can scare the hell out of you. When my wife was hooked up to a fetal monitor during her first labor, we were comforted by the sound of the baby's steady, 140-beats-per-minute heartbeat. But at one point the heart rate dropped to 120, then 100, then 80, then 60. Nothing was wrong—the doctor was just trying to turn the baby over—but hearing her little heart slow down that much nearly gave my wife and me heart attacks.

A final word of advice about fetal monitors: if you absolutely have to have one, make sure they turn the volume down (better yet, all the way off).

Cesarean Section

A ll things being equal, most parents would prefer to bring their babies into the world "normally." And most of the time, things go the way they're supposed to. But when they don't, the chances of having a Cesarean section delivery increase greatly. In fact, more than 30 percent of all children born in hospitals are delivered by C-section.

What She's Going Through

Most childbirth preparation classes (see pages 102–6) put a great deal of emphasis on natural, unmedicated deliveries. Many women, therefore, feel a tremendous amount of pressure to deliver vaginally, and may actually consider themselves "failures" if they don't—especially after they've invested many hours in a painful labor (for more on this see pages 159–60).

In addition, recovering from a Cesarean is much different than recovering from a vaginal birth (see page 160 for more details). My wife (and I) spent three nights in the hospital after the C-section delivery of our first daughter. But after our second daughter was born (vaginally), we remained in the hospital for only five hours. (We rushed it a little; most people stay twenty-four to forty-eight hours after a vaginal birth.)

What You're Going Through

Your take on the C-section is undoubtedly going to be quite different from your partner's. Researcher Katharyn May found that only 8 percent of men whose partners delivered by C-section objected to the operation; 92 percent were "greatly relieved." Although I didn't participate in this study, it accurately reflects my own experience. It simply had never occurred to me that we might somehow have "failed" when our first daughter was delivered by C-section. On the contrary, I remember feeling incredibly thankful that my wife's suffering would finally end. And seeing how quickly and painlessly the baby was delivered made me wonder why we hadn't done it sooner.

Despite the relief a father may feel on his wife's behalf, a C-section can be a trying experience for him. As a rule, he is separated from his wife while she is being prepped for surgery, and he is not given any information about what's happening. I remember being left in the hall outside the operating room, trying to keep an eye on my wife through a tiny window. Besides being terribly scared, I felt completely helpless—and useless—as the doctors, nurses, and assistants scurried around, blocking my view, getting dressed, washing, opening packages of scalpels, tubes, and who knows what else. Only one person— the pediatrician who would attend the delivery—took a minute to pat me on the shoulder and tell me that everything would be all right. I've never felt more grateful to another person in my life.

When I was finally permitted into the operating room, I was told—no discussion allowed—to sit by my wife's head. There was a curtain across her chest that prevented me from seeing what the surgeons were doing. Whenever I stood up to get a better view the anesthesiologist shoved me back down into my seat. I was too exhausted to argue, but a friend of mine whose partner had a C-section in the same hospital a few years later *did* argue and was able to go around to the "business end" of the operation.

Staying Involved

My friend and I may be the lucky ones; in many hospitals men aren't allowed into the operating room at all. Others permit them in only if they've taken a special C-section class. Hopefully, even before you check in you and your partner will have already told your OB exactly what your preferences are should there be a C-section, and you'll be familiar with any relevant hospital policies. (See pages 16–17 for other things to discuss with your OB.)

Don't forget that although a C-section is a fairly commonplace operation, it is still major surgery. And after the operation, your partner will need some extra special care.

Common Medical Reasons for a Cesarean Section

♦ **Fetopelvic disproportion.** The mother's pelvis is too small to allow the baby's head to pass through the vagina.

♦ **Failure of the labor to progress.** Exhausted by an excessively long labor, the mother is unable to push the baby out.

♦ **Maternal herpes (active).** If the mother has an outbreak of herpes within about four weeks of the birth, there isn't much choice.

♦ **Placenta problems.** *Abrupto placenta* (separation of the placenta from the uterine wall before labor begins) causes bleeding and can threaten the lives of both mother and baby. *Placenta previa* (the placenta is fully or partially blocking the opening of the cervix) prevents the baby from leaving the uterus.

♦ **Position of baby.** Under certain circumstances, if the baby is breech (coming out feet first) or transverse (facing in the same direction as the mother instead of facing backward), a C-section may be more likely.

♦ **Previous C-section birth(s).** Contrary to popular belief, having had one C-section increases the chances of subsequent C-sections by only about 3 percent. Most women with a prior C-section have V-BACs (vaginal births after Cesarean).

First of all, as strange as it may sound, after having a C-section your partner may feel terribly left out. She will have been fully awake during the operation and will be anxious to meet the new baby. But whereas after a vaginal birth the mother gets to see and touch the baby immediately, after a C-section the baby is usually quickly whisked away to have his or her lungs suctioned out. (Although it may seem like a scary emergency procedure, suctioning a C-section baby's lungs is quite routine. In a vaginal birth, as the baby passes through the birth canal, he or she gets what amounts to a natural Heimlich maneuver that squeezes the amniotic fluid out of the lungs. C-section babies need a little help.)

You'll probably get to make a "ceremonial" umbilical cord cut (the surgeons will have already cut the cord while delivering the baby). If the baby is being cared for right in the delivery room, make sure to tell your partner exactly what's happening—she'll want to know. In some hospitals, C-section babies are removed from the delivery room immediately after the birth and

Some of the Most Common Nonmedical Reasons for a Cesarean Section

♦ **Scheduling.** Doing a C-section delivery means your doctor won't have to wait around for an unpredictably long labor.

♦ **It's easier.** Many OBs consider C-sections safer than vaginal deliveries.

♦ **It's Friday.** More operations are performed on Friday afternoons, when tired doctors are eager to get home for the weekend, than at any other time of the week.

♦ **Fear of lawsuits.** If something goes wrong with the birth—fetal or maternal distress, or even a birth defect—the obstetrician is likely to be blamed for having let the labor go on too long. In some cases, therefore, OBs perform a C-section to speed things up.

taken straight to the nursery, where they're washed, examined, and put through basically the same procedures covered in the preceding chapter. This whole process can take anywhere from a few minutes to a few hours.

Although you might want to remain with your partner and comfort her immediately after the delivery, stay with your baby instead. It's bad enough for a newborn to be deprived of snuggling with one of his parents right away, but it would be worse if the baby couldn't be with *either* of you. Staying with our daughter also eased my paranoia that she might be switched in the nursery (a highly unlikely occurrence, given the rather elaborate security measures in place in most hospitals).

Your Partner's Emotional Recovery

Having an unplanned C-section can trigger a whole host of conflicting emotions in your partner. She, like you, may feel greatly relieved that the pain is over and the baby is safe. At the same time, it's very natural for her to second-guess herself and the decision she made, to start wondering whether there was anything she could have done to avoid the operation, or to believe she's failed because she didn't deliver vaginally. These feelings are especially common when the C-section was performed because labor "failed to progress" (meaning that the cervix wasn't dilating as quickly as the doctors may have thought it should).

If you sense that your partner is experiencing any of these negative emotions, it's important for you to counter them immediately. She really needs to know that no one could have done more, or been stronger or braver than

> ## Facts to Remember about Recovery from a Cesarean Section
>
> ♦ Your partner's incision will be tender or downright painful for at least several days. Fortunately, she'll undoubtedly be receiving some intravenous pain medication.
>
> ♦ The nursing staff will visit quite frequently to make sure that your partner's uterus is getting firm and returning to its proper place, to see whether she's producing enough urine, and to check her bandages.
>
> ♦ Your partner will have an IV until her bowels start functioning again (usually one to three days after delivery). After the IV is removed, she'll start on a liquid diet, then add a few soft foods, and finally return to her normal diet.
>
> ♦ Your partner will need to get up and move around. Despite the fact that a C-section is major abdominal surgery, less than twenty-four hours after the delivery the nurses will probably encourage—and help—your partner to get out of bed and take a couple of rather painful-looking steps.
>
> ♦ Before your partner leaves the hospital the sutures or staples will be removed. Yes, staples. Until I heard the clink as the doctor dropped them into a jar, I'd just assumed that my wife had been sewn up after her C-section.

she was; that she didn't give in to the pain too soon; that she tried everything she could have to jump start a stalled labor; and that the decision she made (or at least agreed to) was the best one—both for the baby and for herself.

Some of these thoughts might seem obvious to you—so obvious that you might think they don't need to be said at all. But they do—especially by you. You were there with her and you know better than anyone else exactly what she went through. So, being comforted and praised by you will mean a lot more to her than hearing the same words from a well-meaning relative.

An Important Warning

Never, never, never suggest to your pregnant partner that she consider a C-section—let your doctor make the first move.

When my wife was pregnant with our second daughter, the pain she had been through during her first labor and delivery was still fresh in my mind. At one point I told her that I was really upset by the thought that she might

have to endure another horrible labor, and I suggested that she should consider a C-section.

I had no idea that someone could get so furious so quickly. Even though
I had the very best intentions and was sincerely thinking only of her and how
to minimize her pain, she thought I was being completely insensitive. Clearly,
I had underestimated how incredibly important giving birth vaginally—especially after already having had one C-section—was to her.

Many of the men I've talked to have had similar thoughts about making the
C-section suggestion to their partners. Most of them were wise enough not to
act on their impulse. And hopefully, you won't either. Telling your partner
how you're feeling and what you're going through is, in most cases, the right
thing to do. But when it comes to C-sections, really and truly, it's an issue
that's just too hot to handle.

Notes:

Gee Honey, Now What Do We Do?

What She's Going Through

Physically

- Vaginal discharge (called *lochia*) that will gradually change from bloody to pink to brown to yellow over the next six weeks or so
- Major discomfort if there is an episiotomy or C-section incision (the pain will disappear over the next six weeks)
- Constipation
- Breast discomfort—starting on about the third day after the birth (when her breasts become "engorged" with milk), and if she's breastfeeding, her nipples will probably be sore for about two weeks
- Gradual weight loss
- Exhaustion—especially if her labor was long and difficult
- Continued contractions—especially while breastfeeding—but disappearing over the next several days
- Hair loss (most women stop losing hair while they're pregnant, but when it's over, they make up for unlost hair)

Emotionally

- Relief that it's finally over
- Excitement, depression, or both (see page 163)
- Worried about how she'll perform as a mother, and whether she'll be able to breastfeed (but over the next few weeks, her confidence will build and these worries should disappear)
- A deep need to get to know the baby
- Impatience at her lack of mobility
- Decreased sex drive

Postpartum Blues and Depression

About 70 percent of new mothers experience periods of mild sadness, weepiness, mood swings, sleep deprivation, loss of appetite, inability to make decisions, anger, or anxiety after the baby is born. These postpartum blues, which many believe are caused by hormonal shifts in a new mother's body, can last for hours or days, but in most cases they disappear within a few weeks. If you notice that your partner is experiencing any of these symptoms, there's not much you can do except be as supportive as possible. Encourage her to get out of the house for a while and see to it that she's eating healthily.

In a small number of cases, postpartum blues can develop into postpartum depression. According to the American College of Obstetricians and Gynecologists, postpartum depression, if not recognized and treated, may become worse or last longer than it needs to. Here are some symptoms to watch out for:

- Postpartum blues that don't go away after two weeks, or feelings of depression or anger that surface a month or two after the birth.
- Feelings of sadness, doubt, guilt, helplessness, or hopelessness that begin to disrupt your partner's normal functioning.
- Inability to sleep when tired, or sleeping most of the time, even when the baby is awake.
- Marked changes in appetite.
- Extreme concern and worry about the baby—or lack of interest in the baby and/or other members of the family.
- Fear of harming the baby or thoughts of self-harm.

Again, most of what your partner will go through after the birth is completely normal and nothing to worry about. So be patient, and don't expect her to bounce back immediately. If you're really concerned, however, encourage your partner to talk with you about what she's feeling and to see her doctor or a therapist.

What's Going On with the Baby

For thousands of years, most people have believed that at birth, infants were capable only of eating, sleeping, crying, and some rudimentary movements. But in the mid-1960s researchers Peter Wolff and Heinz Prechtl discovered that infant behavior they had previously thought to be random actually fell into six clearly defined states that are apparent within just a few minutes after a baby is born. "By recognizing them and realizing when they occur and what the expected responses are in each," write Marshall and Phyllis Klaus, authors of *The Amazing Newborn,* "parents not only can get to know their infants but also can provide most sensitively for their needs." Here's a summary of the six states, based on the Klauses' book.

Quiet Alert

Babies in the quiet alert state rarely move—all their energy is channeled into seeing and hearing. They can (and do) follow objects with their eyes and will even imitate your facial expressions.

Within the first hour of life, most infants have a period of quiet alertness that lasts an average of forty minutes. During his or her first week, the normal baby spends only about 10 percent of any twenty-four-hour period in this state. It is in this state, however, that your baby is most curious and is absorbing information about his or her new world. And while the baby is in this state you will first become aware that there's a real person inside that tiny body.

Active Alert

In this state, the baby will make small sounds and move his or her arms, head, body, face, and eyes frequently and actively.

The baby's movements usually come in short bursts—a few seconds of activity every minute or two. Some researchers say these movements are designed to give parents subtle clues about what the baby wants and needs. Others say these movements are just interesting to watch, and therefore promote parent/infant interaction.

Crying

Crying is a perfectly natural—and for some, frequent—state (for more on this, see pages 181–85). The infant's eyes may be open or closed, the face red, and the arms and legs moving vigorously.

Often, just picking up the baby and walking around with him or her will stop the crying. Interestingly, researchers used to think that babies were soothed by the upright position. It turns out, though, that what makes them stop crying is the *movement toward* the upright position.

Keep in mind, too, that crying is *not* a bad thing—it not only allows the baby to communicate but also provides valuable exercise. So, if your efforts to calm him or her aren't immediately successful (and the baby isn't hungry or stewing in a dirty diaper), don't worry; chances are the tears will stop by themselves in a few minutes.

Drowsiness

This is a transition state that occurs as the baby is waking up or falling asleep. There may still be some movement, and the eyes will often look dull or unfocused.

Leave the baby alone—let him or her drift off to sleep or move into one of the alert stages.

Quiet Sleep

The baby's face is relaxed and the eyelids are closed and still. There are no body movements and only tiny, almost imperceptible mouth movements.

When your baby is in the quiet sleep state, you may be alarmed at the lack of movement and be afraid the baby has stopped breathing. If so, lean as close as you can and listen for the baby's breath. Otherwise, *gently* put a hand on the baby's back and feel it rise and fall. Try to resist the urge to wake the baby up—most newborns spend up to 90 percent of their first few weeks sleeping.

Active Sleep

Eyes are usually closed, but may occasionally flicker open. The baby may also smile or frown, make sucking or chewing movements, and even whimper or twitch—just as adults do in their active sleep state.

Half of a baby's sleep time is spent in quiet sleep, the other half in active sleep, with the two states alternating in thirty-minute shifts. So, if your sleeping baby starts to stir, whimper, or seems to be waking up unhappy, wait a few seconds before you pick him or her up to feed, change, or soothe. If left alone, the baby may very well slip back into the quiet sleep state.

Newborn babies are capable of a lot more than crying, sleeping, and looking around. Just a few hours out of the womb, they are already trying to communicate with those around them. They can imitate facial expressions, have some control over their bodies, can express preferences (most prefer patterned objects to plain objects and curved lines to straight ones), and have remarkable memories. Marshall Klaus describes playing a game with an eight-hour-old girl in which he asked one colleague (who was a stranger to the baby) to hold her and slowly stick out her tongue. After a few seconds, the baby imitated the woman. Then Dr. Klaus took the baby and passed her around to twelve other doctors and nurses who were participating in the game, all of whom were told not to stick their tongues out. When the baby finally came back to the first doctor, she—without any prompting—immediately stuck out her tongue again. Even at just a few hours old, she had obviously remembered her "friend."

If you want your baby to respond to and play with you, try to establish communication during his or her active alert stage. (During the first few months infants are particularly responsive to high contrast, and so black-and-white toys and patterns are often a big hit.) But be patient. Babies are incredibly bright little creatures, but they also have minds of their own. This means that despite your best efforts, your baby may not be interested in performing like a trained seal whenever you wish.

What You're Going Through

Unconditional Love

Sooner or later, almost every writer takes a crack at trying to describe love. And for the most part, they fall short. But there's a line in Maurice Sendak's classic children's book *Where the Wild Things Are* that captures the feeling of loving one's own child exactly: "Please don't go—we'll eat you up—we love you so." As crazy as it may sound, that's precisely what my love for my daughters feels like to me. Whether we're playing, reading a book, telling each other about our days, or I'm just gazing at their smooth, peaceful faces as they sleep, all of a sudden I'll be overcome with the desire to pick them up, mush them into tiny balls, and pop them in my mouth. I know, it sounds nuts, but just you wait.

One of my biggest fears during my wife's second pregnancy was that I wouldn't be able to love our second child as much as the first—that there wouldn't be enough of the consuming, overpowering love I felt for our first daughter to share with the new baby. But I really had nothing to worry about. Three seconds after our second daughter was born, I already wanted to eat her up, too.

Awe at What the Female Body Can Do

Watching your partner go through labor is truly a humbling experience; chances are, your own physical courage, strength, and resolve have rarely been put to such a test. But there's nothing like seeing a baby come out of a vagina to convince you that women are really different from men.

I know that vaginal birth has been around for millions of years and that that's the way babies are supposed to be born. Yet in a strange way, there's something almost unnatural about the whole process—the baby seems so big and the vagina so small (it kind of reminds me of the ship-in-a-bottle conun-drum). Ironically, a C-section somehow seems more "normal": when the fetus is full-grown, cut an appropriately sized exit and let the baby out. You'd think that with all the technological advances we've made in other areas, we'd have invented an quicker, easier, less painful way to have children.

Jealousy

"The single emotion that can be the most destructive and disruptive to your experience of fatherhood is jealousy," writes Dr. Martin Greenberg in *The Birth of a Father.*

There's certainly plenty to be jealous about, but the real question is "Whom are you jealous of?" Your partner for being able to breastfeed and for her close relationship with the baby, or the baby itself for taking up more than his or her "fair share" of your partner's attention, and for having full access to your partner's breasts while you aren't even supposed to touch them? The answer is "both."

Now that that the baby's born, communication with your partner is even more important than before. Jealousy's "potential for destruction," writes Greenberg, "lies not in having the feelings but in burying them." So if you're feeling jealous, tell her about it. But if you can't bring yourself to discuss your feelings on this issue with your partner, take them up with a male friend or relative. You'll be surprised at how common these feelings are.

Feeling Pushed Away or Left Out

Another common feeling experienced by new fathers is that of being pushed away or excluded from the new parenting experience. "The mother plays a critical role," writes Pamela Jordan. "She can bring her mate into the spotlight or keep him in the wings. The most promoting mothers . . . brought their mates into the experience by frequently and openly sharing their physical sensations and emotional responses. They actively encouraged their mates to share the experience of becoming and being a father."

While it's easy to give in to your feelings of jealousy, throw up your hands, and leave the parenting to your partner, don't do it. Encourage her to talk about what she's feeling and thinking, and ask her specifically to involve you as much as possible.

A good way to cut down on your potential feelings of jealousy or of being pushed away is to start getting to know your baby right away—even before you leave the hospital. Change as many diapers as you can (if you've never changed one before, get one of the nurses to show you how), give the baby a sponge bath, or take him or her out for a walk while your partner gets some rest.

Amazement at How Being a Parent Changes Your Life

It's virtually impossible to try to explain the myriad ways becoming a parent will change your life. You already know you'll be responsible for the safety and well-being of a completely helpless person. You've heard that you'll lose a little sleep (all right, a lot) and even more privacy. And you've prepared yourself for not being able to read as many books or see as many movies as you did before. These are some of the big, obvious changes, but it's the tiny details that will make you realize just how different your new life is from your old one.

The best way I can describe it is this: Sometimes one of my daughters will put some food into her mouth and after a few chews change her mind, take it out, and hand it to me. Most of the time I take the offering and pop it into my mouth without a second thought. You probably will too. Even more bizarre, since I became a father I have actually had serious discussions with my friends about the color and consistency of the contents of my children's diapers. So will you.

Bonding with the Baby

No one knows exactly where or when it started, but one of the most widespread—and most enduring—myths about child rearing is that women are somehow more nurturing than men and are therefore better suited to parenting.

In one of the earliest studies of father-infant interaction, researcher Ross Parke made a discovery that might shock the traditionalists: the fathers were just as caring, interested, and involved with their infants as the mothers were, and they held, touched, kissed, rocked, and cooed at their new babies with at least the same frequency as the mothers did. Several years later, Dr. Martin Greenberg coined a term, *engrossment,* to describe "a father's sense of absorption, preoccupation, and interest in his baby."

Parke and a number of other researchers have repeatedly confirmed these findings about father-infant interaction, and have concluded that what triggers engrossment in men is the same thing that prompts similar nurturing feelings in women: early infant contact. "In sum," writes Parke, "the amount of stimulatory and affectional behavior depends on the opportunity to hold the infant."

But What If I Don't Bond Right Away?

Although we've spent a lot of time talking about the joys of loving your child and how important it is to bond with the infant as soon as possible, many new fathers (and mothers, for that matter) *don't* feel particularly close to the new baby immediately after the birth.

In a way, this really makes more sense than the love-at-first-sight kind of bonding you hear so much about. After all, you don't even know this new little person. He or she may look a lot different than you expected. And, if your partner's labor and delivery were long and arduous, you may unconsciously be blaming the baby for the difficulties or may simply be too exhausted to fully appreciate the new arrival.

So, if you haven't established an instant attachment with your baby, there's absolutely nothing wrong with you. And, more important, there's no evidence whatsoever that your relationship with or feelings for your child will be any less loving than if you'd fallen head over heels in love in the first second. Just take your time and don't pressure yourself.

Staying Involved

The First Few Days
In the first few days you're going to have to learn to juggle a lot of roles. You're still a lover and friend to your partner, and, of course, you're a father. But for now, your most important role is that of support person to your partner. Besides her physical recovery (which we'll talk more about below), she's going to need time to get to know the baby and to learn (if she chooses to) how to breastfeed.

When our first daughter was born (by C-section), the three of us spent four days in the hospital (which meant three uncomfortable nights on a crooked cot for me). But when our second daughter was born (vaginally), we all checked out less than five hours after the birth. In both cases, though, my first few days at home were mighty busy—cooking, shopping, doing laundry, fixing up the baby's room, getting the word out, screening phone calls and visitors, and making sure everyone got plenty of rest.

Coming Home . . . and Beyond
Within a few minutes after we'd brought our first daughter home from the hospital, my wife and I looked at each other and almost simultaneously asked, "Well, now what are we supposed to do?" An important question, no doubt, and one that seems to come up time and time again.

A NOTE ON RECOVERY
As far as the baby is concerned, there's not much to do in the beginning besides feeding, changing, and admiring him or her. But your partner is a different

story. Despite everything you've heard about women giving birth in the fields and returning to work a few minutes later, that's not the way things usually happen. Having a baby is a major shock to a woman's system. And, contrary to popular belief, the recovery period after a vaginal birth is not necessarily any shorter or easier than the recovery period after a C-section. In fact, my wife—who has delivered both ways—says recovering from the C-section was a lot easier.

Whatever kind of delivery your partner has, she'll need some time— probably more than either of you think—to recover fully. According to a recent study, more than 40 percent of new mothers experience fatigue and breast soreness in the first month after giving birth. In addition, vaginal discomfort, hemorrhoids, poor appetite, constipation, increased perspiration, acne, hand numbness or tingling, dizziness, and hot flashes are common for a month after delivery. And between 10 and 40 percent of women feel pain during sexual intercourse, have respiratory infections, and lose hair for three to six months.

Helping the Other Kids Adjust to Their New Sibling

Handling your older children's reactions to their new baby brother or sister requires an extra touch of gentleness and sensitivity. Although kids are usually wildly excited (initially, at least) at their new status as big brother or big sister, most of them will have some adjustment problems later on—as soon as they realize that the new kid is more than just a temporary visitor. My older daughter, for example, who was completely potty trained before her sister was born, regressed and began wetting her bed again a few weeks after we brought our younger daughter home. She also began making increased demands for our attention—demands we weren't always able to satisfy.

One way to help your older children adjust to their new sibling is to make them feel involved from the start. Our older daughter stayed at my parents' house while my wife was in labor with our younger daughter. But as soon as the baby was born, we called our older daughter and told her first. She then got to be the one to make the announcement to the other members of the family that she was a big sister. We also had her come to the hospital right away (even though it was past her bedtime), where she got to hold her new sister "by herself." Later, allowing her to "help" diaper, bathe, feed, and clothe her little sister really made her feel like the baby was "hers."

"Is There Anything We Can Do?"

One of the most common questions you'll hear from people is whether they can help out in any way. Some people are serious, others are just being polite. You can tell one group from the other by keeping a list of chores that need to be done and asking them to take their pick.

One of the nicest, and most helpful, things that was done for us both times we brought a baby home was a group effort by some of our friends. They'd gotten together and, taking turns, brought us meals every day for more than a week. Not having to cook or shop gave us a lot more time to spend together and let us get some rest. And of course, when our friends had their children, we were there with our spinach lasagna and a bottle of wine.

Do You *Really* Want Your Mother-in-law to Move in with You Right after the Birth?

Be careful about having people stay over to help with the newborn—especially parents (yours or hers). The new grandparents may have more traditional attitudes toward parenting and may not be supportive of your involvement with your child. They may also have very different ideas about how babies should be fed, dressed, carried, played with, and so on. If you do have someone stay with you to help out after the birth, make sure they understand that you and your wife are the parents and that what you say ultimately goes.

"Not so fast. I want to be called 'Nana.'"

Here are some things you can do to make the recovery process as easy as possible and to start parenting off on the right foot.

- Help your partner resist the urge to do too much too soon.
- Take over the household chores or ask someone else to help. And if the house is a mess, don't blame each other.
- Be flexible. Expecting to maintain your normal, prefatherhood schedule is unrealistic—especially for the first six weeks after the birth.
- Don't allow your relationship with your partner to be based solely on your child. If she's up to it, go on a date with your partner and leave the baby with a relative or friend.
- Be patient with yourself, your partner, and the baby. You're all new at this.
- Be sensitive to your partner's emotions. Recovery has an emotional component as well as a physical one.
- Make sure to get some time alone with the baby. You can do this while your partner is sleeping or, if you have to, send her out for a walk.
- Control the visiting hours and the number of people who can come at any given time. Dealing with visitors takes a lot more energy than you might think. And being poked, prodded, and passed around won't make the baby very happy. Also, for the first month or so, ask anyone who wants to touch the baby to wash his or her hands first.
- Keep your sense of humor.

Immediate Concerns . . . with Long-term Impact

FEEDING THE BABY: BREAST VS. BOTTLE

In the fifties and sixties—when most people reading this book were born—breastfeeding was out of style and most women our mothers' age were given a wide variety of reasons (by their doctors, of course) not to breastfeed. But in the nineties you'd be hard-pressed to find anyone who doesn't advocate breastfeeding. Even in the medical community, there's general agreement that breastfeeding is just about the best thing you can do for your child.

If you and your partner haven't already decided to breastfeed, here are the reasons why you should:

FOR THE BABY

- Breast milk provides exactly the right balance of nutrients needed by your newborn. In addition, breast milk contains several essential fatty acids that are not found in baby formula.

♦ Breast milk adapts, as if by magic, to your baby's changing nutritional needs. Neither of our children had a single sip of anything but breast milk for the first seven or eight months of life, and they're both incredibly healthy kids.

♦ Breastfeeding greatly reduces the chance that your baby will develop food allergies. If your family (or your partner's) has a history of food allergies, you should withhold solid foods for at least six months.

♦ Breastfed babies are less prone to obesity in adulthood than formula-fed babies. This may be because with the breast, it's the baby—not the parent—who decides when to quit eating.

♦ Breastfed babies have a greatly reduced risk of developing respiratory and gastrointestinal illness.

♦ Breastfeeding is thought to transmit to the infant the mother's immunity to certain diseases.

FOR YOU AND YOUR PARTNER

♦ It's convenient—no preparation, no heating, no bottles or dishes to wash . . .

♦ It's free. Formula can cost a lot of money.

♦ It gives your partner a wonderful opportunity to bond with the baby. In addition, breastfeeding will help get your partner's uterus back into shape and may reduce her risk of ovarian and breast cancer.

♦ In most cases there's always as much as you need, and never any waste.

♦ Your baby's diapers won't stink. It's true. Breastfed babies produce stool that—at least compared to "real food" stools—doesn't smell half bad.

A Note on Juice

If you and your partner decide not to breastfeed, or decide to supplement breastfeeding with a bottle, don't fill it with juice. A recent study found that children who drink large quantities of fruit juice—especially apple juice—suffer from frequent diarrhea and, in the worst cases, may fail to grow and develop normally. The problem is that babies love juice so much that, if you give them all they want, they'll fill up their tiny stomachs with it, leaving no room for the more nutritious foods they need. The American Dietetic Association recommends that parents refrain from giving their babies juice until they're at least six months old, and then restrict juice intake until age two.

A Special Note on Breastfeeding

As natural as breastfeeding is, your partner and the baby may need anywhere from a few days to a few weeks to get the hang of it. The baby won't immediately know how to latch on to the breast properly, and your partner—never having done this before—won't know exactly what to do either. This initial period, in which cracked and even bloody nipples are not uncommon, may be quite painful for your partner. And with the baby feeding six or seven times a day, it may take as long as two weeks for your partner's nipples to get sufficiently toughened up.

Surprisingly, your partner won't begin producing any real milk until two to five days after the baby is born. But there's no need to worry that the baby isn't getting enough food. Babies don't eat much the first 24–48 hours, and any sucking they do is almost purely for practice. Whatever nutritional needs your baby has will be fully satisfied by the tiny amounts of *colostrum* your partner produces. (Colostrum is a kind of premilk that helps the baby's immature digestive system get warmed up for the task of digesting real milk later.)

Overall, the first few weeks of breastfeeding can be very stressful for your partner. If this is the case, *do not* be tempted to suggest switching to bottles. Instead, be supportive, praise her for the great job she's doing, bring her something to eat or drink while she's feeding, and encourage her to keep trying. You also might want to ask your pediatrician for the name of a local lactation consultant (yes, there really is such a thing).

SLEEPING ARRANGEMENTS

Your pediatrician will probably tell you that your baby should get used to sleeping by him- or herself as soon after birth as possible. The reasoning is that in American culture we emphasize early independence, so babies should adapt quickly to being away from their parents—especially if both parents work and the children are in day care.

But there is another school of thought that maintains that babies should sleep in the same bed as their parents (an idea shared by about 80 percent of the world's population). The rationale is that human evolution simply can't keep pace with the new demands our culture is placing on its children. "Proximity to parental sounds, smells, heat, and movement during the night is precisely what the human infant's immature system expects—and needs," says James McKenna, an anthropologist and sleep researcher.

If You Decide to Share Your Bed with Your Child

Do it because you and your partner *want* to, not because you feel you
have to. You're not negligent or overindulgent parents for doing it, so
don't be embarrassed by your choice. But remember: no waterbeds—
a baby could roll between you and the mattress. Also, overly soft mattresses and pillows may pose a risk of suffocation.

If Family Sleeping *Isn't* for You

Don't feel guilty. You're not a bad or selfish parent for not doing it.
Teaching your children to be independent does not mean that you don't
have a close bond with them. But don't feel like a failure if you allow
an occasional exception, such as when a child is ill or has had a fright-
ening experience.

So which approach is right? Well, given the wide divergence of expert opin-
ions out there, it's a tough call—one you'll ultimately have to make on your
own. Our older daughter slept in a bassinet in our room for a month or so until
we moved her into her own room. Our younger daughter, however, slept in bed
with us for six months before moving to her own room. Neither of them had
any trouble making the transition, or any sleep problems thereafter.

Here are a few of the most common questions you're likely to have if you
haven't already decided where your child will be sleeping.

- **How will it affect the baby's independence?** There's absolutely
  no agreement on this. Richard Ferber, author of *Solve Your Child's Sleep
  Problems,* maintains that "sleeping alone is an important part of a child's
  learning to be able to separate from his parents without anxiety and
  to see himself as an independent individual." In contrast, Thomas F.
  Anders, M.D., a professor of psychiatry, contends that "every child is
  born with a strong need for lots of close physical contact with a caregiver, and children in whom this need isn't met early in their lives may
  end up trying to fill it as adults."
- **What about safety?** Most adults—even while asleep—have a highly developed sense of where they are. After all, when was the last time you fell
  out of bed? So, the risk of accidentally suffocating your baby is pretty slim.
- **How will the baby sleep?** Despite what you might think, co-sleeping
  children tend to sleep more *lightly* than children who sleep alone

(blankets rustling and parents turning over in bed wake them up). But light sleeping isn't necessarily a bad thing. In fact, there seems to be a correlation between lighter sleep and a lower incidence of SIDS (Sudden Infant Death Syndrome).

Sharing a bed with your infant not only affects your child, but it can also have a serious impact on you. You'll lose a lot of sexual spontaneity, and you may also lose some sleep. Even the soundest-sleeping kids generally wake up every three or four hours; 70 percent of them just look around for a few minutes and soothe themselves back to sleep. But if your baby is in the other 30 percent, he or she may wake up, see you, and want to play.

A Note on Middle-of-the-Night Wake-ups

If your baby wakes up in the middle of the night hungry, and your partner is breastfeeding, you might as well stay in bed and let your partner take care of things. I know that doesn't sound terribly gallant, but, really and truly, there's not much you can do to help. And your sleeping through the 2 A.M. feeding may actually benefit your partner. Whenever I was able to get a full night's sleep, I was fairly fresh for the 7 A.M. child-care shift, allowing my wife a few more precious hours in bed.

If, however, your baby is being bottle-fed (either with formula or expressed breast milk), you should do your fair share of the feedings. You might want to work out a system in which the one who does the 2 A.M. feeding gets to sleep in (or gets breakfast in bed, or whatever).

Sometimes, though, your baby might wake up at two or three in the morning for no other reason than to stay awake for a few hours and check things out. In this kind of situation, you and your partner can either split the child-entertainment duty or stay up together and see what's on late-night TV; if there were any sitcoms or detective shows you missed when you were growing up, you can probably catch the reruns at three in the morning. Thanks to my older daughter's middle-of-the-night awakenings, my wife and I once had the rare opportunity to see what may have been (hopefully) the only episode of "David Cassidy, Teen Detective."

SEX AFTER THE BABY

Most doctors advise women to refrain from intercourse for at least six weeks after giving birth. But before you mark that date on your calendar, remember that the "six-week rule" is only a guideline. Resuming intercourse ultimately depends on the condition of your partner's cervix and vagina, and, more important, on how you're both feeling. It's not uncommon for couples to take as long as six months to fully reestablish their prepregnancy sex life.

Many factors influence when and how a couple decides to resume their sex life. Here are a few:

♦ When you had sex with your partner before, she was the woman you loved. Now, she's also a mother—a thought that reminds many men of their own mothers and can be a big turn-off. Several studies have shown that many women, too, have a tough time reconciling their roles as lover and mother, and may see themselves as unsexual.

♦ According to Dr. Jerrold Shapiro, some men have "emotional difficulty being sexual with the part of their wives that produced their children." While I can't say that seeing my daughter coming out of my wife's vagina was particularly erotic, I always found the sight of her feeding our babies rather arousing.

♦ In the first few weeks after the birth, your partner may focus more on the baby than on you.

♦ You might be jealous of the baby and his or her intimate relationship with your partner.

♦ You may feel especially aroused at having concrete proof (the baby) of your virility.

Chances are, you were fairly abstinent during the last few weeks of the pregnancy and you can hardly wait to get your sex life back on track. But you should expect the first few times you have sex after the baby is born to be a period of tentative rediscovery for both of you. Her body has changed, and she may respond differently than she used to. She may still be worried that having sex will hurt, and you may be afraid of the same thing. Go slowly, take your cues from her, and give yourselves plenty of time to get used to each other again.

You may also find that your partner's vagina is much drier than before, making intercourse painful. This doesn't mean she isn't aroused by you; it's simply a common postbirth occurrence—especially if she's breastfeeding. If this happens, invest in a little K-Y jelly, Astroglide, or other similar lubricant.

CHILD CARE

With more and more women entering the work force, it's getting harder to find a traditional dad-goes-to-work-while-mom-stays-at-home kind of family anymore, and it's nearly impossible to find the mom-goes-to-work-while-dad-stays-at-home variety. And even if you or your partner wanted to be a full-time caregiver, you probably couldn't afford it anyway. So, sooner or later, most couples find themselves considering some form of child care.

IN-HOME CHILD CARE

More than 1.4 million children are cared for in their homes during the day by nonrelatives, and another 500,000 are cared for by live-in help.

In-home care is convenient; you don't have to worry about day-care schedules, and your baby can stay in the environment to which he or she has become accustomed. In addition, your baby will receive individual attention, and, if you stay on top of the situation, the caregiver will keep you up to date on your child's development. Finally, by remaining at home your child will be less exposed to germs and illness.

Every time my wife and I have tried to find in-home child care, it has been a traumatic experience. But the first time was the hardest. Besides being afraid that the person we chose would turn out to be an ax murderer, we were worried that no one else could love our daughter as much or care for her as well as we did. While nothing can replace a parent's love, there are many wonderful caregivers out there who can give your baby the next best thing. You just need to know how to find them.

The most common ways to find in-home care are:
♦ Agencies
♦ Word of mouth
♦ Bulletin boards (either caregivers respond to your ad, or you respond to theirs)

The first thing to do is to conduct thorough interviews over the phone— this will enable you to screen out the obviously unacceptable candidates (for example, the ones who are only looking for a month-long job, or those who don't drive if you need a driver). Then invite the "finalists" over to meet with you, your partner, and the baby in person. Make sure the baby and the prospective caregiver spend a few minutes together, and pay close attention to how they interact. My wife and I ruled out a couple of people because they showed absolutely no interest in holding, cuddling, or playing with the baby. And we hired one woman largely because the moment she walked in the door she picked up our daughter and started playing with her. Be sure to get—and check—references (it's awkward, but absolutely essential). Ask each of the references why the baby-sitter left his or her previous jobs, and what the best and worst things about him or her were. Also, make sure to ask the prospective caregiver the questions listed on the following page.

Questions to Ask Prospective Caregivers

 • What previous child-care experience have you had (including caring for younger relatives)?
 • What age children have you cared for?
 • Tell us a little about your own childhood.
 • What would you do if . . . (give several examples of things a child might do that would require different degrees of discipline).
 • How would you handle . . . (name a couple of emergency situations).
 • Do you know baby CPR? (If not, you might want to consider paying for the caregiver to take a class.)
 • What are your favorite things to do with kids?
 • Do you have a driver's license?
 • What days/hours are you available/not available? How flexible can you be if an emergency arises while we're at work?
 • Are you a native speaker of any foreign language?

Other Important Topics to Cover

 • Compensation (check with other people who have caregivers for the going rate) and vacation.
 • Telephone privileges.
 • Complete responsibilities of the job: feeding, bathing, diapering, changing clothes, reading to the baby, and so on, as well as what light housekeeping chores, if any, will be expected while the baby is sleeping.
 • English-language skills—particularly important in case of emergency (you want someone who can accurately describe to a doctor or 911 operator what's going on).
 • Immigration/green card status

You might want to draw up an informal contract, listing all of the caregiver's responsibilities—just so there won't be any misunderstandings.

When you make your final choice, have the person start a few days before you return to work so you can all get to know each other, and so you can spy.

A NOTE ABOUT LIVE-IN HELP

Hiring a live-in caregiver is like adding a new member to the family. The process for selecting one is similar to that for finding a non-live-in caregiver, and you can use most of the questions listed on this page when conducting

What to Look for in a Day-care Center

- The level of training of the staff. Some have degrees in early childhood education; some aren't much more than warm bodies.
- Safety: windows, fences around yards, access to kitchen appliances and utensils (knives, ovens, stoves, household chemicals, and so forth).
- Is it licensed by the National Association of Education and Child Care?
- Overall cleanliness.
- Caregiver/child ratio. (In California, one licensed caregiver can take care of as many as four infants. I personally think that any more than two is too many.)
- Quality, condition, and number of toys.
- Security: what precautions are taken to ensure that kids can be picked up only by the person you select? Do strangers have access to the center?

Before you make your final choice, be sure to take a tour. Spend half an hour or so—when all the kids are there—observing. Are the children happy? Are they doing the kinds of activities you expected?

Finally, in the weeks after you pick the perfect day-care center, make a few unannounced visits—just to see what goes on when there aren't any parents around.

interviews. After you've made your choice, you might want to try out your new relationship on a non-live-in basis for a few weeks, just to make sure everything's going to work out to your satisfaction.

OUT-OF-HOME CHILD CARE

Many people—even those who can afford in-home child care—feel that out-of-home centers are preferable. For one, a good day-care center is, as a rule, much better equipped than your home and offers your child a wide range of stimulating activities. In addition, out-of-home day care gives your child the opportunity to play with other children; this, in the opinion of many experts, helps children become better socialized and more independent. The downside, of course, is that interacting with other kids usually means interacting with their germs—children in out-of-home day care get sick a lot more often than those cared for at home.

Taxes and Child Care

♦ Be sure to get your caregiver or baby-sitter's social security number; you'll need it to take advantage of the tax deduction/credit for child-care expenses.

♦ If you pay a baby-sitter or other household worker more than $1,250 a year, you are required to deduct social security taxes. The amount you need to deduct changes every year, so check with the Social Security Administration or your accountant to be sure.

CRYING

Let's face it, babies cry; it's their job. The fact is that 80 to 90 percent of all babies have periods of crying that can last from twenty minutes to an hour *every day.* Still, there's nothing like holding an inconsolably crying child to make even the most seasoned parent feel inadequate.

I think fathers tend to feel this sense of inadequacy more acutely than mothers, perhaps because most men have been socialized to view themselves as less than fully equipped to care for children and therefore have less than complete confidence in their parenting abilities.

When (not if) your child starts to cry, resist the urge to hand him or her to your partner. She knows nothing more about crying babies than you do (or will soon enough). To start with, however, here are a few things you can do to reduce the amount of time your child will spend crying:

♦ **Take note of what your partner eats while breastfeeding.** After one horrible, agonizing evening of inexplicable crying from our usually happy baby and a frantic call to the doctor, we discovered that the broccoli my wife had eaten for dinner was the culprit.

♦ **Know your baby.** Within just a few days after birth, your baby will develop distinct cries: "I'm tired," "Feed me now," "Change my diaper," "I'm uncomfortable as can be," "I'm bored in this car seat," and "I'm crying because I'm mad and I'm not going to stop no matter what you do." Once you learn to recognize these cries, you'll be able to respond appropriately and keep your baby happy. It's also important to know your child's routine—some babies like to thrash around and cry a little (or a lot) before going to sleep, others don't.

♦ **Carry your baby more.** Some studies show that the more babies are held (even when they're not crying), the less they cry.

After you've tried soothing, feeding, changing the diaper, checking for loose diaper pins or uncomfortable clothing, and rocking, the baby may still continue to howl. Sometimes there's really nothing you can do about it (see the section on coping, pages 183–85), but sometimes all it takes is a new approach. Here are a few alternatives you might want to try:

- **Hold the baby differently.** Not all babies like to be held facing you; some want to face out so they can see the world. One of the most successful ways I've learned to soothe a crying baby—and I've tried this on many kids besides my own—is to use Dave's Magic Baby Hold. (Dave, the father of a close friend, supposedly used the Hold to calm his own three children.) Quite simply, have the baby "sit" in the palm of your hand—thumb in front, the other fingers on the baby's bottom. Then have the baby lie face down on the inside of your forearm, with his or her head resting on the inside of your elbow. Use your other hand to stroke or pat the baby's back.
- **Distraction.** Offer a toy, a story, a song. If the baby is diverted by a story or song, you'd better be prepared to repeat it over and over and over . . .
- **Give the baby something to suck on.** Just take a guess why they call them "pacifiers." If you don't approve of pacifiers, you can either help the baby suck on his or her own fingers, or loan out one of yours.
- **Give the baby a bath.** Some babies find warm water soothing. Others freak out when they get wet. If you do decide to try bathing a crying infant, don't do it alone. Holding onto a calm soapy baby is no easy chore. But keeping a grip on a squirming, screaming, soapy baby takes a team of highly trained specialists.
- **Invest in a frontpack.** A lot of crying babies just want to be held all the time, and no matter how strong you think you are, your arms—and back—won't last forever. You'll be able to use your frontpack for other purposes as well—both my daughters traveled hundreds of miles strapped to my chest, while I did my cross-country ski-machine workout. In addition, carrying the baby around in the pack might give you an inkling of what it was like for your partner to be pregnant.
- **Take the baby for a walk or a drive.** A word of caution: this doesn't work for all babies. When she was an infant, my elder daughter would fall asleep in the stroller or the car in a heartbeat. But my younger daughter hates riding in the car, especially when she's tired, and cries even more when she's put in her car seat. If you don't feel like going out, try putting the baby on top of a running washing machine or dryer. There's also a special device called SleepTight that, when attached to

the baby's crib, simulates the feel (and sounds) of a car going fifty-five miles an hour. Call 1-800-NO-COLIC for more information.

COPING WITH CRYING

If you've tried everything you can think of to stop the baby from crying, but to no avail, here are some things that may help you cope:

- **Tag-team crying duty.** There's no reason why both you and your partner have to suffer together through what Martin Greenberg calls "the tyranny of crying." Spelling each other in twenty-minute or half-hour shifts will do you both a world of good. Getting a little exercise during your "time off" will also calm your nerves before your next shift starts.

- **Let the baby "cry it out."** If the crying goes on for more than twenty minutes or so, try putting the baby down in the crib and letting him or her cry. If the screaming doesn't stop after ten or fifteen minutes, pick the baby up and try a different approach for another fifteen minutes or so. Repeat as necessary.

"I'm worried about him. He's not picking at his food."

A Note on Crying in Public

Dealing with a crying child in public was particularly stressful for me.
It wasn't that I didn't think I could handle things; rather, I was embarrassed by and afraid of how other people would react. Would they think I
was hurting the baby? Would they call the police? If they did, how could
I possibly prove that the baby was mine? Fortunately, no one ever called
the police, but there was no shortage of comments, which ranged from
the seemingly helpful ("Sounds like that baby is hungry") to the blatantly
sexist and demeaning ("Better get that baby home to her mother").

Although my fears about my children crying in public may sound a
little paranoid (okay, a lot), I know I'm not alone. Just about every father
I've spoken to has had similar thoughts in similar situations. I have to
admit, however, that most of the women I've mentioned this to (including
my dear wife) think I'm completely nuts on this point.

Colic

Starting at about two weeks of age, some 20 percent of babies develop
colic—crying spells that, unlike "ordinary" crying, can last for hours at
a time, sometimes even all day or all night. The duration and intensity of
crying spells peaks at around six weeks and usually disappears entirely
within three months.

Since there's no real agreement on what causes colic or on what to do
about it, your pediatrician probably won't be able to offer a quick cure.
Some parents, however, have been able to relieve (partially or completely) their colicky infants with an over-the-counter gas remedy for
adults. Talk to your doctor about whether he or she thinks taking this
medication would benefit your child.

♦ **Get some help.** Dealing with a crying child for even a few minutes can
provoke incredible rage and frustration. And if the screams go on for
hours, it can become truly difficult to maintain your sanity, let alone
control your temper. If you find yourself concerned that you might lash out
(other than verbally) at your child, call someone: your partner,
pediatrician, parents, baby-sitter, friends, neighbors, clergy person, or
even a parental-stress hotline. If your baby is a real crier, keep these
numbers handy.

♦ **Don't take it personally.** Your baby isn't deliberately trying to antagonize you. It's all too easy to let your frustration at this temporary situation permanently interfere with the way you treat your child. "Even if your powerful feelings don't lead to child abuse," write the authors of *What to Expect the First Year*, "they can start eroding your relationship with your baby and your confidence in yourself as a parent unless you get counseling quickly."

PLAYING WITH YOUR BABY

Playing with your child is one of the most important things you can do with him or her. Kids learn just about everything they need to know from playing. Besides, it's fun for you. Some studies indicate that babies who are played with a lot tend to be more attentive and interactive as they grow up, and retain these qualities later in life as well.

As a rule, men and women have different play styles: men tend to stress the physical, high-energy type of playing; women, the social and emotional. Neither kind of parent-child interaction is better—each is different *and* indispensable, and there's no point in trying to compare or rate them.

Several researchers have done extensive studies on the impact of physical play on children and have come up with some interesting conclusions. Ross Parke, for example, found that girls who are exposed to higher than traditional levels of physical play become more assertive in their peer interactions later in life—this is a particularly important finding to those of us who are concerned by all the recent studies showing that our daughters may be shortchanged in their education because they don't speak up in class as often as boys.

In general, babies love physical play, and by the time they're just a few days old, they've already learned which of their parents will play with them which way—and they'll react accordingly. Here are some important things to keep in mind about playing:

♦ **Use moderation.** It's perfectly fine to play with a baby as young as a few days old, but restrict each session to five minutes or so. Too much playing can make your child fussy or irritable.

♦ **Take your cues from the baby.** If he or she cries or seems bored, stop what you're doing.

♦ **Schedule your fun.** The best time for physical play is when the baby is in the active alert state; playing with toys or books is fine during the quiet alert state (see page 164). Also, choose a time when your full attention can be devoted to the baby—no phone calls or other distractions.

Finally, don't play too vigorously with the baby immediately after feeding. Believe me—I learned the hard way.

+ **Get comfortable.** Find a place where you can get down to the baby's level—preferably on your back or stomach on the floor or bed.

+ **Be patient.** As mentioned above, your baby is not a trained seal—don't expect too much too soon.

+ **Be encouraging.** Use lots of facial and verbal encouragement—smiles, laughter. Although the baby can't understand the words, he or she definitely understands the feelings. Even at only a few days old, your baby will want to please you, and lots of encouragement will build his or her self-confidence.

+ **Be gentle—especially with the baby's head.** Because babies' heads are relatively large (one-quarter of their body size at birth vs. one-seventh by the time they're adults) and their neck muscles are not yet well devel-

---

A Note on Dressing Children

Getting a baby dressed is not an easy task; their heads always seem too big to go through the appropriate openings in their shirts, and their hands regularly refuse to come out of the sleeves. There are a few things you can do to make dressing a little easier:

+ Reach through the sleeve and pull your baby's hands through— it's a lot easier than trying to shove from the other side.

+ Buy pants or overalls whose legs snap open. Some manufacturers make baby clothes that are absolutely beautiful but impossible to put on or take off. The snap-open legs also make diaper changing much easier—you don't have to remove the whole outfit to access the diaper.

Also, don't overdress your baby. For some strange reason, people tend to bundle their children up in all sorts of blankets, sweaters, hats, and gloves—even in the summer. But unless you're Eskimos, there's no reason to dress your children like one. A basic rule of thumb is to have the baby wear the same kind of clothes you do, plus a hat. Layering clothing is sometimes a good way to go—if the baby gets too hot, you can remove a layer.

Finally, remember this simple rule: "If they can't walk, they don't need shoes." It's not only a waste of money, but confining a baby's feet in a hard pair of shoes all day long can actually damage the bones.

oped, their heads tend to be pretty floppy for the first few months. Be sure to support the head—from behind—at all times, and avoid sudden or jerky motions.

A COUPLE OF WARNINGS

- *Never* shake your child. This can make their little brains rattle around inside their skulls, causing bruises or permanent injuries.
- *Never* throw the baby up in the air. Yes, your father may have done it to you, but he shouldn't have. It looks like fun but can be extremely dangerous.

Notes:

Fathering
Today

For the first weeks and months after the birth of your child, you'll be spending much of your time in the role of support person for your partner. But after a while, you'll settle into a more "normal" life—one and/or both of you will go back to work, and you might feel like taking in a movie or visiting some friends. And gradually, you'll be figuring out exactly what it means to be a father and how involved you intend to be in your child's life. Do you want to be someone he or she runs to when hurt or sad? Will you know his shoe size or whether she likes pants that zip up or slip on? Will you schedule any medical appointments or play dates, or will you leave those things to your partner?

Whatever you decide, you'll soon come face-to-face with the fact that being a father in America—especially an *involved* one—is going to be tough. Sure, the responsibilities of the job itself are difficult and at times frustrating, but the biggest obstacles you'll face—ones you've probably never even thought about before—are societal.

Only recently have men and women felt able to speak out against the traditional role fathers have played in the family. And only recently has society finally recognized that the distant father is not the ideal father. But in the midst of this newfound freedom to lash out against yesterday's absent, neglectful fathers, today's fathers are falling victim to old stereotypes.

According to one stereotype, men haven't taken an active role in family life because they haven't wanted to. But is this true of today's fathers? Hardly. Many of us realize that the traditional measures of success are not all they're cracked up to be, and we are committed to being a major presence in our children's lives, physically and emotionally. The hitch is that society (and by this I mean all of us) not only won't support us but actively discourages us. Quite simply, Americans don't value fatherhood nearly as much as motherhood. (Even the words have different associations: motherhood is equated

P. Steiner
THE WASHINGTON TIMES

with caring, nurturing, and love, whereas *fatherhood* connotes merely a biological relationship.) As a result, men are rarely accepted if they assume a
different role than the one they are "supposed" to assume.

The emphasis on traditional roles starts long before you might imagine.
Even before they can walk, children of both sexes are bombarded with the
message that fathers are basically superfluous. Just think of the books your
parents read to you, and that you'll probably read to your own children. Have
you ever noticed that there aren't any fathers in *The Cat in the Hat; Where
the Wild Things Are; Are You My Mother?; Goodnight Moon; The Runaway
Bunny;* and *Peter Rabbit?*

In the vast majority of children's books, a woman is the only parent, while
the man—if he appears at all—comes home late after work and bounces baby
around for five minutes before putting her to bed. My local library has a special catalog of children's books with positive female characters—heroines and
mothers. As a father who shares the child-care responsibilities equally, I find

it extremely frustrating that the library doesn't have a catalog (or even many books) with positive male role models.

In recent years there's been a push to portray more accurately the roles that women and minorities play in shaping our country's history and culture. *Little Black Sambo,* for example, has all but disappeared from library and bookstore shelves, and most new children's books make a conscious effort to take female characters out of the kitchen and the nursery and give them professional jobs and responsibilities. But one group—fathers—continues to be portrayed in the same stereotypical mold as always.

One of my older daughter's favorite books, for example, is *Mother Goose and the Sly Fox,* "retold" by Chris Conover. It's the story of a single mother (Mother Goose) with seven tiny goslings who is pitted against (and naturally outwits) the Sly Fox. Fox, a neglectful, and presumably unemployed, single father, lives with his filthy, hungry pups in a grimy hovel littered with the bones of their previous meals. Mother Goose, a successful entrepreneur with a thriving lace business, still finds time to serve her goslings homemade soup in pretty porcelain cups. The story is funny and the illustrations marvelous, but the unwritten message is that women take better care of their kids than men, who have nothing else to do but hunt down and kill innocent, law-abiding geese.

You'll find the same negative portrayals of fathers in the majority of children's classics. Once in a great while someone will complain about *Babar*'s colonialist slant (you know, little jungle dweller finds happiness in the big city and brings civilization—and fine clothes—to his backward village). But you'll never hear anyone ask why Babar is automatically an "orphan" after his mother is killed by the evil hunter. Why can he find comfort only in the arms of another female? Why do Arthur and Celeste's mothers come alone to the city to fetch their children? Don't the fathers care? Do they even have fathers?

If books were the only place children got messages about the way the world is supposed to be, it might be possible to edit out the negative messages. But sooner or later most kids find themselves in front of some kind of a screen—movie or television—and the most common images of fathers they're likely to see are nearly identical to those perpetuated in print: if fathers are there at all, they're usually fairly useless.

One of the best examples of the negative father image—and the effect it has on our children—is *Bambi,* which, although about fifty years old, is still one of the most popular children's movies of all time. In the early part of the film, Bambi enjoys a warm, nurturing relationship with his mother. And it's not until about halfway through the movie that we learn he has a father—a stern, authoritative, and, at best, fleeting presence in the young deer's life.

At the end of the movie, Bambi himself becomes a father, and, like the only male role model he's ever known, does his fathering from a distant hill.

As significant as movie images are to children, by far the most powerful delivery system for negative portrayals of fathers is the small screen. The average American child spends eight hours a day watching television—a lot more time than he or she spends reading. Clearly, then, the images of fathers that children—and adults—get from television have the potential to do much more damage than the images they get from books.

Overall, men get a pretty raw deal when it comes to the way they're portrayed on television. Frederic Hayward, the director of Men's Rights Inc., in Sacramento, California, conducted a survey of a thousand random TV advertisements and found that "100 percent of the jerks singled out in male-female relationships were male. There were no exceptions. . . . 100 percent of the ignorant ones were male. 100 percent of the incompetent ones were male." And for fathers, the negative portrayals run a little deeper. Besides being depicted as dumber than their wives and children, fathers—if they're part of the commercial family unit at all—are shown as oblivious to the needs of their children. Mothers, it seems, are the only ones who care. Here are a few examples:

- In a spot for Post Raisin Bran, a father and his daughter are oohing and aahing about their cereal. "Somebody must really love us," says Dad. "Who do you think it is?" "Mommy!!!" yelps the child.
- Another breakfast cereal, Kix, is billed as being "Kid tested, Mother approved."
- When it comes time to make lunch, advertisers insist that "Choosy mothers choose Jif."
- In a nationally run magazine ad, Fisher-Price gleefully informs us that "it took Fisher-Price and 2,043 mothers to design a highchair like this."
- In a commercial for Aquafresh toothpaste, a father and child are arguing about whether fluoride or mouthwash is the toothpaste's most important ingredient. They probably would have argued all day, if Mom hadn't stepped in to tell them, "You need both."
- A certain cough medicine is "recommended by Dr. Mom."

And when it comes to what's shown between the commercials, fathers don't fare a lot better. While there are a few exceptions, most fathers in sitcoms are portrayed as buffoonish, easily outwitted men whose main contribution to their families is money (just think of "The Simpsons" and "Married—With Children"). While it's possible to argue that mothers still do most of the shopping and

SIPRESS

feeding, the subtle yet critical message contained in these ads is that fathers simply don't care. They don't feed their kids, don't clothe them, and won't be there to take care of them when they're sick. Mothers are the better parents and fathers play, at best, a secondary role in the home.

It seems that we've confused men's lack of training in child care with a lack of interest in or concern about their children. A lot of today's fathers— who, like Bambi, were raised in "traditional" families—simply had no role models, no one to teach them the skills they lack today.

This brings up an interesting contradiction. Many supposedly open-minded people are quick to put the blame on "socio-economic pressures" when discussing hot issues such as crime and drugs. But when discussing fathers' purported indifference toward their children, no one thinks to hold society responsible. Instead, we're told by someone as highly respected as Barbara Jordan, a former congresswoman and advisor to the governor of Texas, "Women have a capacity for understanding and a compassion which a man structurally does not have. . . . He's just incapable of it." When various fathers' rights groups protested her remarks, Jordan defended them, saying they were "based on observable fact." Imagine what would happen if a man had made a similarly inflammatory statement about women. Or African Americans. Or anyone except a man.

Perhaps the most active way we have of discouraging men's involvement with children is by continually portraying men as dangerous. In an article I wrote for the *New York Times Magazine,* I described an incident that took place not along ago. I was pushing my older daughter on the swing at our favorite park, when I heard a little girl start to scream. She was just a few feet away, teetering on the small platform at the top of a long, steep slide. As I watched, she lost her grip on the handrail and began to fall. Without thinking, I leapt over to the slide, caught the girl, and set her down on the sand. I knelt down and was about to ask her if she was all right, when a woman picked the girl up, gave me a withering look, and hustled the child away. "Didn't I tell you not to talk to strange men in the park?" the woman asked her daughter, glaring over her shoulder at me. "Did he hurt you?"

I remember standing there for a few seconds, stunned, as the woman bundled her child into the car and drove off. I wondered what she had been thinking. Hadn't she seen me playing with a happy girl who called me Daddy? It was a cloudless, summer day and as I looked around the park, I realized I was the only man there. That was when it hit me: I—the father—was invisible. What had come to that woman's mind was what was most ingrained and automatic—the stereotyped images of a man in the park, menacing and solitary.

In some twisted way, I can understand these "instinctive" fears. If I'd turned around and seen a strange man kneeling near my daughter, I might have jumped to the worst possible conclusions, too. And when my wife and I interview baby-sitters for our daughters, *I* am the one who has the most serious qualms about hiring a man for the job.

But my "understanding" of these fears is based less on the truth about how men actually *are* with children than on how we've been trained to *view* men with children. I still remember the "safety movies" I saw in about the third or fourth grade—scary images of the sinister, mustachioed men (and they were always men) lurking behind trees in the park or trying to entice us into their cars.

I'm not saying that there aren't some sick men out there, men who do horrible things to children. Men are the perpetrators in most sexual abuse cases (which constitute 11 percent of all cases of abuse and neglect). Yet there are plenty of sick women out there too; women murder more children than men do and are the perpetrators in the majority of physical and psychological abuse cases.

None of this, of course, is meant to imply that men are just hapless victims, or that all the obstacles fathers face are "someone else's" fault. In fact, some of the most significant barriers have been erected by men themselves. In the workplace, for example, where men still occupy the majority of positions of power, men who try to take time off work to be with their families—either as paternity leave or by reducing their work schedules—find that their employers abuse them, treat them like wimps, and question how serious they are about their jobs (see pages 88–92 for more on this).

Despite the many obstacles, some of us have risked our careers and jeopardized our finances to try to break through the "glass ceiling" that keeps us at work—and away from our families. But in many cases, when we finally get home we run into another barrier—this one imposed by none other than our partners.

Here's an all-too-common scenario: When I was visiting some friends not long ago, their six-month-old son started fussing. Colin, who was holding the baby, began rocking him. Suddenly his wife, Marina, appeared and whisked the baby away. "Let me take him, honey," she said. "I think I know what he needs."

I've seen scenes of this kind played out many times before (and not only at Colin and Marina's house), but this time I began to wonder. Did Marina really know what the baby needed? And if so, did she know better than Colin did?

According to a significant amount of research, the answers to my questions are "probably" and "no," respectively. In a variety of studies, researcher Ross Parke found that fathers—despite stereotypes to the contrary—are just as sensitive and responsive to their infants' needs as mothers. They know when something is wrong, and they take appropriate action. So why then, had Colin—a man I knew wanted an active role in raising his children—simply handed his crying son over to his wife? When you factor out sheer laziness from the equation, the answer to that question is a little tougher. What it seems to boil down to is that most of us—men as well as women—simply assume that women know more about kids than men.

In some ways, that may be true. On average, women do spend more time taking care of children than men do, and their skills may be a little sharper than men's. But parenting skills are not innate—they are learned through experience and training. No first-time parents, mothers or fathers, know instinctively how to soothe a colicky baby or prevent diaper rash. In fact, when our older daughter was born, my wife was taught how to breastfeed by a *male* nurse.

Still, the stereotypes persist, and to a great extent women control the amount—and quality—of time men spend with their children. Although most mothers feel that fathers should play an important role in the kids' lives, that role should be "not quite as important as mom's," according to a nationwide survey of mothers, published as *The Motherhood Report: How Women Feel about Being Mothers.* In fact, researchers found that two out of three women seem threatened by equal participation and may themselves be "subtly putting a damper on men's involvement with their children because they are so possessive of their role as primary nurturer."

It may sound as though all these obstacles are almost too numerous to overcome. Well, there may be a lot of them, and they may be quite ingrained, but if you're willing to put in the time and effort, you'll be able to have—and maintain—an active, involved relationship with your children.

Here are some things you can do:

♦ **Get some practice.** Don't assume that your partner magically knows more than you do. Whatever she knows about raising kids, she's learned by doing—just like anything else. And the way you're going to get better is by doing things, too. Research has shown, for example, that the lack of opportunity may be one of the biggest obstacles to fathers' being more affectionate with their children. As mentioned in the preceding chapter, once they get to hold them, fathers are at least as affectionate with their children—cooing, looking at, holding, rocking, soothing—as their partners are. (So much for the stereotype about men being emotionally distant by nature.)

♦ **Take charge.** Ultimately, if you don't start taking the initiative, you'll never be able to assume the child-rearing responsibilities you want—and deserve. In all the times I've seen women pluck crying or smelly babies from their husbands' arms, I've never heard a man say, "No, honey, I can take care of this." So, if you find yourself in a situation like that, try a few lines such as: "I think I can handle things" or "That's okay; I really need the practice." And there's also nothing wrong with asking her for advice—you both have insights that the other could benefit from. But have her tell you instead of doing it for you.

♦ **Don't devalue the things you like doing with the kids.** As discussed in the preceding chapter, men and women generally have different ways

of interacting with their children; both are extremely important to your child's development. So don't let anyone tell you that wrestling, playing "monster," or other so-called guy things are somehow not as important as the "girl things" your partner may do (or want you to do).

♦ **Get involved in the day-to-day decisions that affect your kids' lives.** This means making a special effort to share with your partner such responsibilities as meal planning, food and clothes shopping, cooking, taking the kiddies to the library or bookstore, getting to know their friends' parents, and planning play dates. Not doing these things can give the impression that you don't think they're important or that you're not interested in being an active parent. And by doing them, you make it more likely that your partner will feel comfortable and confident in sharing the nurturing role with you. But try to log some private, "quality" time with the kids, too. Sure, somebody has to schlepp the kids all over town—to doctor appointments, ballet lessons, or soccer practice—but that shouldn't be the only contact you have with them.

♦ **Keep communicating.** If you don't like the status quo, let your partner know. But be gentle. If at first she seems reluctant to share the role of child nurturer with you, don't take it too personally. Men are not the only ones whom society has done a bad job of socializing. Many women have been raised to believe that if they aren't the primary caregivers (even if they work outside the home as well), they've somehow failed as mothers. If your partner does work outside the home, you might want to remind her of what Karen DeCrow, a former president of the National Organization for Women (NOW), says: "Until men are valued as parents, the burden of childrearing will fall primarily to women and frustrate their efforts to gain equality in the workplace."

◆ **If you're in a position to do something for other men, do it.** All things being equal, try hiring a male baby-sitter once in a while. Or consider asking a male friend instead of the usual women friends to do some baby-sitting when you and your wife want a night out. If you need to ease yourself into it, try the teenage son of some friends. Continuing not to trust men and boys will continue to make men and boys think of themselves as untrustworthy and will make it difficult for them to be comfortable enough in their role as parent to take on as much responsibility as they—and their partners—would like.

◆ **Get your partner to be your publicist.** Pamela Jordan writes that "men tend not to be perceived as parents in their own right by their mates, co-workers, friends or family. They are viewed as helpmates or breadwinners." The cure? "The mother can mitigate the exclusion of the father by others by including the father in the pregnancy and parenting experiences and actively demonstrating her recognition of him as a key player," Jordan says.

◆ **Get some support.** Even before your baby is born, you're likely to become aware of the vast number of support groups for new mothers. It won't take you long to realize, however, that there are few, if any, groups for new fathers. And if you find one, it will probably be geared toward men whose contact with their kids is limited to five minutes before bedtime.

After having read this book, you know that men have just as many pregnancy, birth, and child-rearing questions as their partners. So, if you can't find a new fathers' support group in your own neighborhood, why not be a trailblazer and start one of your own?

Here are a few ways you might get going:

◆ Start meeting regularly with male friends who already have kids. Talk on the phone, go for walks with the kids, meet in a park for lunch.

◆ Encourage other expecting male friends or new fathers to join you, and ask them to contact their male friends who have or are about to have children.

♦ Put up signs in local children's clothing and/or toy stores.

♦ Check with your partner's doctor, your pediatrician, and your childbirth class instructor about helping you advertise your group.

♦ Contact the Y or some of the local family-planning agencies to see if they'll help with publicity.

♦ Check with the people who organize some of the new mothers' groups— maybe they'd be interested in a fathers' auxiliary.

Who knows—if you do a good enough job publicizing your new fathers' group, you might even be able to turn it into a real business. Don't laugh: plenty of people are making money on mothers' groups.

A Final Word

Throughout this book we've talked about the benefits—both to you and to your children—of your being an active, involved father, and about how fatherhood actually begins long before your first child is born. What we haven't touched upon, though, is the positive effect your fatherhood role can have on your relationship with your partner.

Sociologist Pepper Schwartz has found that couples who worked *together* to raise their children "seemed to create a more intimate and stable relationship. They did more together. They talked on the phone together much more and spent more child-related time together. Wives in the study said they believed that raising children together created a more intimate adult relationship." Other research confirms Schwartz's findings. For example, a 1993 study showed that fathers who were actively involved with their children had a much lower divorce rate than those who weren't.

So it's in everyone's best interest for you to do everything you possibly can to become an involved father. It's not easy, but the rewards—for you, your children, and your partner—are incalculable.

Selected
Bibliography

Books

American College of Obstetricians and Gynecologists. *The ACOG Guide to Planning for Pregnancy, Birth, and Beyond.* Washington, D.C.: ACOG, 1990.

Beail, N., and J. McGruire, eds. *Fathers: Psychological Perspectives.* London: Junction Books, 1982.

Bitman, S., and S. Zalk. *Expectant Fathers.* New York: Hawthorn Books, 1978.

Bradley, Robert A. *Husband Coached Childbirth.* New York: Harper and Row, 1974.

Cath, H. C., A. Gurwitt, and L. Gunsberg, eds. *Fathers and Their Families.* Hilldale, N.J.: Analytic Press, 1989.

Colman, L. L., and A. D. Colman. *Pregnancy: The Psychological Experience.* New York: Noonday Press, 1991.

Cowan, C. P., and P. A. Cowan. *When Partners Become Parents.* New York: Basic Books, 1992.

Eisenberg, A., H. Murkoff, and S. Hathaway. *What to Expect When You're Expecting.* New York: Workman, 1988.

Grad, R., D. Bash et al. *The Father Book.* Washington, D.C.: Acropolis Books, 1981.

Greenberg, Martin. *The Birth of a Father.* New York: Continuum, 1985.

Klaus, M., and P. Klaus. *The Amazing Newborn.* Reading, Mass.: Addison-Wesley, 1985.

Klaus, M., J. Kennel, and P. Klaus. *Mothering the Mother.* Reading, Mass.: Addison-Wesley, 1993.

Lamb, Michael, ed. *The Role of the Father in Child Development.* New York:
John Wiley and Sons, 1981.

Minnick, M. A., K. J. Delp, and M. C. Ciotti. *A Time to Decide, a Time to Heal.*
Mullett Lake, Mich.: Pineapple Press, 1990.

Osherson, S. *Finding Our Fathers: The Unfinished Business of Fatherhood.*
New York: Free Press, 1986.

Paulaha, Dennis. *An American Child's Portfolio.* Edina, Minn.: Patron, 1991.

Pederson, A., and P. O'Mara, eds. *Being a Father.* Santa Fe: John Muir, 1990.

Shapiro, Jerrold L. *The Measure of a Man.* New York: Delacorte, 1992.

———. *When Men are Pregnant.* New York: Delta, 1993.

Thevenin, Tine. *The Family Bed.* New York: Avery, 1987.

Van de Carr, F. R., and M. Lehrer. *Prenatal Classroom.* Atlanta: Humanics
Learning, 1992.

Verny, T., and J. Kelly. *The Secret Life of the Unborn Child.* New York: Delta,
1991.

Verny, T., and P. Weintraub. *Nurturing the Unborn Child.* New York: Delacorte
Press, 1991.

Journal articles

Broude, Gwen J. "Rethinking the Couvade: Cross-Cultural Evidence." *American Anthropologist* 90 (1988): 903–11.

Cummings, David. "The Effects of Miscarriage on a Man." *Emotional First
Aid* 1, no. 4 (1984): 47–50.

Davidson, J. R. "The Shadow of Life: Psychosocial Explanations for Placenta
Rituals." *Culture, Medicine and Psychiatry* 9 (1985): 75–92.

Goldbach, R. C. et al. "The Effects of Gestational Age and Gender on Grief
After Pregnancy Loss." *American Journal of Orthopsychiatry* 61 (July 1991):
461–67.

Jordan, Pamela. "Laboring for Relevance: Expectant and New Fatherhood."
Nursing Research 39 (January–February 1990): 11–16.

Klein, Hillary. "Couvade Syndrome: Male Counterpart to Pregnancy." *International Journal of Psychiatry in Medicine* 21, no. 1 (1991): 57–69.

May, K. A. "Factors Contributing to First-Time Fathers' Readiness for Fatherhood: An Exploratory Study." *Family Relations* 31 (July 1982): 352–61.

———. "First-Time Fathers' Responses to Unanticipated Caesarean Birth:
An Exploratory Study." Unpublished report to U.C.S.F., 1982.

———. "Three Phases of Father Involvement in Pregnancy." *Nursing
Research* 31 (November–December 1982): 337–42.

———. "A Typology of Detachment/Involvement Styles Adopted During

Pregnancy by First-Time Expectant Fathers." *Western Journal of Nursing Research* 2, no. 2 (1980): 445–61.

Miller, W. E. and S. Friedman. "Male and Female Sexuality During Pregnancy: Behavior and Attitudes." *Journal of Psychology and Human Sexuality* 1, no. 2 (1988): 17–37.

Stainton, M. C. "The Fetus: A Growing Member of the Family." *Family Relations* 34 (July 1985): 321–26.

Teichman, Y., and Y. Lahav. "Expectant Fathers: Emotional Reactions, Physical Symptoms and Coping Styles." *British Journal of Medical Psychology* 60 (1987): 225–32.

Zayas, L. H. "Psychodynamic and Developmental Aspects of Expectant and New Fatherhood: Clinical Derivatives from the Literature." *Clinical Social Work Journal* 15 (Spring 1987): 8–21.

———. "Thematic Features in the Manifest Dreams of Expectant Fathers." *Clinical Social Work Journal* 16 (Fall 1988): 283–95.

Resources

Periodicals

American Baby
249 West 17th Street
New York, NY 10011

Child
110 5th Avenue
New York, NY 10011

Family Life
1290 Avenue of the Americas
New York, NY 10104

*Full-Time Dads: The Journal for
Caregiving Fathers*
P.O. Box 577
Cumberland Center, ME 04021

Men's Health
33 East Minor Street
Emmaus, PA 18098

Parenting Magazine
301 Howard Street, 17th Floor
San Francisco, CA 94105

Parents Magazine
685 Third Avenue
New York, NY 10017

Organizations

Men's Health Network
P.O. Box 770
Washington, DC 20044
(202) 543-6461

Men's Issues Think Tank
4839 305th Avenue, N.E.
Cambridge, MN 55008
(612) 689-5885

National Center for Family
Centered Care
7910 Woodmont Avenue, Suite 300
Bethesda, MD 20814
(301) 654-6549
They publish the *National Fathers
Network Newsletter*

National Fathers' Rights
Organization
(414) 798-9000 or (800) 221-2372

Parents, Inc.
270 Commerce Drive
Fort Washington, PA 19034
(215) 628-2402 or (800) 628-2535

Computer networking

America On-Line (800) 522-6364
Has several forums on Parents
Information and Children's Issues.
Look for the keyword "parents"
or "children."

CompuServe (800) 848-8119
Go issues, select "parent connection."

Delphi (800) 544-4005
Type "groups," select "mensnet."

GEnie (800) 638-9636
Type the word "family" (gets you
to the family roundtable); select "1"
for the bulletin board. Choose from
a variety of topics including Parenting, Parenting for school-age kids,
Working parents, For men only.

Internet (USENET) (800) 488-6383
Has several parent- and family-
related news groups, including
clari.news.children, misc.kids, and
clari.news.issues.family.

Prodigy (800) 776-3449
Jump: health, select "health and
life-styles," select "bulletin board,"
select "parenting issues" or
"men's issues"

General information

The Birth and Life Bookstore
141 Commercial Street, NE
Salem, OR 97301
(503) 371-4445
Has an incredible catalog of
childbirth- and parenting-related
books, as well as other resources

Index

taxes and, 181
see also child care
bags, packing for hospital, 121–22
bassinets, 125
bathing, of babies, 182
bathtubs, 127
bed rest, during pregnancy, 137
beds, sharing with infant, 174–76
belly casts, plaster, 88
belly patting, by strangers, 112
bills, 18–22
    for Cesarean section, 20–21
    of hospitals, 20
    for lab expenses, 20
    low-cost alternatives and, 22
    of OB/GYNs, 19–20
    for prenatal testing, 20
    reviewing of, 21
birth announcements, 87, 101–2
birth defects:
    risk factors for, 47
    testing for, 20, 45–47
    in unborn child, dealing with, 49–50
birth plans, 115–18
    sample, 115
    tips for, 118
    topics to cover in, 116–17

births:
    childbirth preparation classes and, 102–7, 156
    essentials to have waiting at home after, 123
    first few days after, 169–72
    going home after, 117
    home as setting for, 13–14
    hospital as setting for, 13
    medicated, 14–15, 108, 116, 151–53, 160
    moment of, 142, 144–45, 148
    mother's recovery from, 169–72
    natural, 14–15, 103, 105, 151, 156
    in planes, trains, and automobiles, 138
    premature, 14, 137
    see also delivery; emergency births; labor
bloody show, 141
books, negative portrayal of fathers in, 189–91
bonding with baby, 168–69
    prenatal communication and, 78–79
bottle feeding, 176
    advantages of breastfeeding over, 172–73
    formula and, 128

Cartoon Credits

About the Authors

Armin A. Brott has written on fatherhood for the *New York Times Magazine, Newsweek,* the *Washington Post, American Baby* magazine, and *Parenting* magazine. He lives with his wife and two daughters in Berkeley, California.

Jennifer Ash is the author of *Private Palm Beach* and a contributing editor to *Town and Country.* She, her husband, and their son make their home in New York City.